COLLECTION EDITOR: **JENNIFER GRÜNWALD**
ASSISTANT EDITOR: **SARAH BRUNSTAD**
ASSOCIATE MANAGING EDITOR: **ALEX STARBUCK**
EDITOR, SPECIAL PROJECTS: **MARK D. BEAZLEY**
SENIOR EDITOR, SPECIAL PROJECTS: **JEFF YOUNGQUIST**
SVP PRINT, SALES & MARKETING: **DAVID GABRIEL**

EDITOR IN CHIEF: **AXEL ALONSO**
CHIEF CREATIVE OFFICER: **JOE QUESADA**
PUBLISHER: **DAN BUCKLEY**
EXECUTIVE PRODUCER: **ALAN FINE**

AVENGERS: TIME RUNS OUT VOL. 2. Contains material originally published in magazine form as AVENGERS #38-39 and NEW AVENGERS #26-28. First printing 2015. ISBN# 978-0-7851-9372-2. Published by MARVEL WORLDWIDE, INC., a subsidiary of MARVEL ENTERTAINMENT, LLC. OFFICE OF PUBLICATION: 135 West 50th Street, New York, NY 10020. **Printed in the U.S.A.** ALAN FINE, EVP - Office of the President, Marvel Worldwide, Inc. and EVP & CMO Marvel Characters B.V.; DAN BUCKLEY, Publisher & President - Print, Animation & Digital Divisions; JOE QUESADA, Chief Creative Officer; TOM BREVOORT, SVP of Publishing; DAVID BOGART, SVP of Operations & Procurement, Publishing; C.B. CEBULSKI, SVP of Creator & Content Development; DAVID GABRIEL, SVP Print, Sales & Marketing; JIM O'KEEFE, VP of Operations & Logistics; DAN CARR, Executive Director of Publishing Technology; SUSAN CRESPI, Editorial Operations Manager; ALEX MORALES, Publishing Operations Manager; STAN LEE, Chairman Emeritus. For information regarding advertising in Marvel Comics or on Marvel.com, please contact Niza Disla, Director of Marvel Partnerships, at ndisla@marvel.com. For Marvel subscription inquiries, please call 800-217-9158. **Manufactured between 1/2/2015 and 2/9/2015 by R.R. DONNELLEY, INC., SALEM, VA, USA.**

10 9 8 7 6 5 4 3 2 1

WRITER: **JONATHAN HICKMAN**

NEW AVENGERS #26
ARTIST: **KEV WALKER**
INK ASSIST: **SCOTT HANNA**
COLOR ARTISTS: **FRANK MARTIN & DONO SANCHEZ ALMARA**
LETTERER: **VC'S JOE CARAMAGNA**
COVER ART: **SALVADOR LARROCA & PAUL MOUNTS**

AVENGERS #38
ARTIST: **STEFANO CASELLI**
COLOR ARTIST: **FRANK MARTIN**
LETTERER: **VC'S CORY PETIT**
COVER ART: **SIMONE BIANCHI**

NEW AVENGERS #27
ARTIST: **SZYMON KUDRANSKI**
COLOR ARTIST: **DONO SANCHEZ ALMARA**
LETTERER: **VC'S JOE CARAMAGNA**
COVER ART: **SALVADOR LARROCA & PAUL MOUNTS**

AVENGERS #39
ARTIST: **MIKE DEODATO**
COLOR ARTIST: **FRANK MARTIN**
LETTERER: **VC'S CORY PETIT**
COVER ART: **ALAN DAVIS, MARK FARMER & BRAD ANDERSON**

NEW AVENGERS #28
ARTISTS: **MIKE DEODATO & MIKE PERKINS**
COLOR ARTIST: **FRANK MARTIN**
LETTERER: **VC'S JOE CARAMAGNA**
COVER ART: **ALAN DAVIS, MARK FARMER & BRAD ANDERSON**

ASSISTANT EDITOR: **JAKE THOMAS**
EDITORS: **TOM BREVOORT WITH WIL MOSS**
AVENGERS CREATED BY STAN LEE & JACK KIRBY

"CAGES"

THE ILLUMINATI

IRON MAN

THE CABAL

BLACK SWAN

PROXIMA MIDNIGHT

CORVUS GLAIVE

TERRAX

VALERIA RICHARDS

DOCTOR DOOM

BENTLEY-23

THE MAD THINKER

MOLECULE MAN

PREVIOUSLY IN NEW AVENGERS
BLACK SWAN. I'M TOLD YOU JUMPED HERE FROM ANOTHER WORLD, THAT YOU HAD SOME KIND OF DEVICE, AND THEN YOU DESTROYED THE PLANET THAT YOU CAME FROM.
THE INCURSIONS BREAK HOPE-- CRUSH WHAT MAKES US DECENT AND STEAL WHAT LITTLE HONOR REMAINS.
I PITY THE THINGS YOU CLING TO--THINKING THIS PROBLEM IS ONE THAT CANNOT BE SOLVED.
I PITY YOU, THINKING YOU HAVE SOME SAY IN HOW ALL THIS ENDS.
EIGHT MONTHS LATER
"THE CABAL IS... UNMANAGEABLE."
IN THE LAST FEW MONTHS WE HAVE DESTROYED EARTH AFTER EARTH, SAVED SCORES OF UNIVERSES.
BUT THEY HAVE LEARNED TO RELISH ATROCITY.
AND SO, NAMOR, YOU COME TO ME FOR HELP...
I THINK NOT.
DOOM IS NO MAN'S SECOND CHOICE.
THE MAD THINKER HAS FOUND A WAY TO FIND OUT WHO IS BEHIND THIS. NOW I HAVE A PLAN, AND ALL THE PIECES TO BRING IT TO PASS...
...THANKS TO THE MOLECULE MAN!
LET THERE BE SUFFERING AND WOE TO ALL WHO STAND IN MY WAY.
WE FINALLY GOT OUR HANDS ON STARK'S DATA. AT FIRST GLANCE, THE WEAPONS FILES APPEAR TO BE...ROBUST.
WE MAY HAVE LOST TONY--
HE'S NOT LOST. WE JUST HAVEN'T FOUND HIM YET.

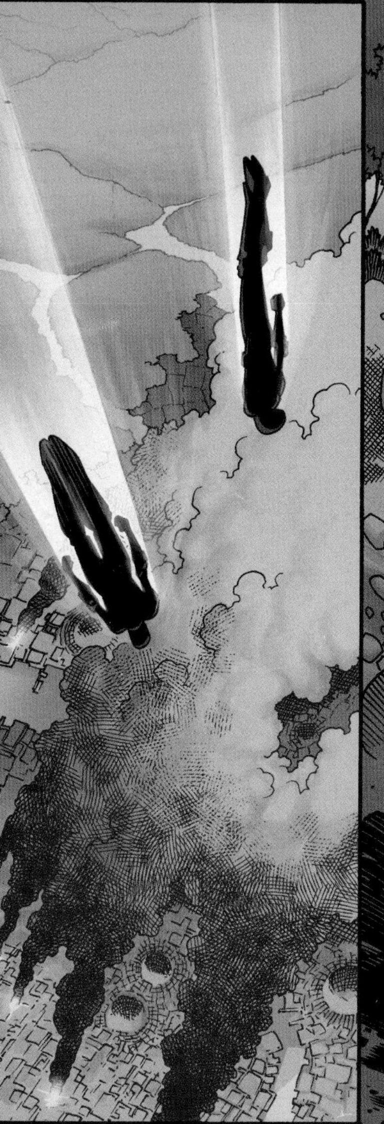

NECROPOLIS.
WAKANDA.

PATIENCE.
PATIENCE IS WHAT IT TAKES IF ONE IS TO ENDURE THE INDIGNITY OF CAPTIVITY.
THE PROBLEM, OF COURSE, WITH PATIENCE IS THAT IT DEMANDS SUBSERVIENCE.
YOU HAVE TO HUMBLE YOURSELF. OVERCOME ONE'S NATURAL INSTINCT TO FIGHT OR FLEE.
DO YOU KNOW WHAT I THINK?
THAT'S ONLY POSSIBLE FOR SOMEONE WHO BELIEVES IN SOMETHING--OR, SPECIFICALLY, SOME*ONE*--TO SUCH AN EXTENT THAT THEY REDUCE THEIR EXISTENCE TO A SECONDARY POSITION.
MY LIFE MEANS NOTHING COMPARED TO RABUM ALAL. I CAN ENDURE ANYTHING FOR HIM.

WHICH IS WHY I DID NOT BREAK...AND YOU WILL.
WHO HAVE YOU EVER SERVED, ANTHONY, BEYOND YOURSELF?

LATVERIA.
BE-DOOP
HELLO?
HELLO, VALERIA.
UGH! FINALLY.
WHAT TOOK YOU SO LONG? I'VE BEEN SITTING HERE WAITING FOR SOM--
IS THAT DOOM?
TELL HIM I HAVE SOME BIG IDEAS WORTH EXPLORING. TRULY DEVIOUS STUFF.

I'M LOOKING FOR AGGRESSIVE PARTNERS...I HAVE FRANCHISE OPPORTUNITIES AVAILABLE!
PRIVATE CONVERSATION, BENTLEY. UNDERSTAND?
PRIVATE!
I HAVE PLANS, VAL!
PLANS!
GLORIOUS PLANS!
HE'S GONE NOW, UNCLE DOOM.
SORRY. YOU KNOW WHAT THEY SAY ABOUT FRIENDS.
YES, VALERIA, EVERYONE NEEDS A FEW. FOR AT TIMES THEY CAN BE...
USEFUL.
DO YOU KNOW WHY I'VE CALLED?
UH, I HAVE A PRETTY GOOD IDEA.
WORLDS COLLIDING. EVERYTHING ENDING...
IS THAT WHERE YOU WANNA START?

HAVE YOU SPOKEN WITH YOUR FATHER ABOUT THIS?
NO. I THINK MOM'S PLAYING THINGS SAFE.
BUT BEFORE HE DISAPPEARED, HE GOT ME A COPY OF ALL HIS DATA. I'VE STUDIED IT, AND COME TO SOME CONCLUSIONS...
I'M GUESSING BY NOW HE KNOWS WHAT THEY ARE.
HOW ABOUT YOU, UNCLE DOOM... YOU WANNA KNOW WHAT I THINK?
YES.
THEN I'LL TELL YOU THE SAME THING I TOLD HIM:
YOU CAN'T WIN.
WHAT YOU HAVE TO DO IS START FIGURING OUT HOW **NOT TO LOSE.**

"HOW NOT TO LOSE..."
WHAT DOES SHE MEAN?
TRULY OMINOUS THINGS, THINKER...
BUT THAT'S NOT OUR CURRENT CONCERN.
IN FACT, IT MATTERS LITTLE WHAT SHE, OR HER FATHER, OR ANY OF THOSE OTHER SO-CALLED GREAT MINDS BELIEVE...
THEIR CURRENT CONCLUSIONS ARE IRRELEVANT--AS THEIR GOALS ARE NOT NECESSARILY OUR OWN.
OPEN THE CHAMBER.
DID YOU SEE IT, VICTOR? HOW THEY COLLAPSED...
DID YOU SEE THE *SHAPE* OF IT?
HAVE YOU SLEPT, MISTER REECE?
LIKE AN OBJECT AT REST.
FREE FROM EXTERNAL CONSTRAINT.
AND DID YOU *DREAM?*

YES. ALWAYS THE SAME DREAM.
ALWAYS THE SAME.
TIME AND TIME AND TIME AGAIN.
I'M REPEATING MYSELF NOW BECAUSE THERE'S LESS OF ME.
TELL ME.
I DREAMT OF SYMMETRY.
OF THE SHAPE OF WHAT'S WAITING FOR US OUT THERE. OF WHAT'S LOOMING IN THE ETHER.
WE HAVE TO STOP IT, VICTOR.
CAN IT BE STOPPED? CAN YOU STOP IT?
CAN YOU SAVE ME? US? ALL OF US?
I BELIEVE I CAN...
BUT I REQUIRE YOUR ASSISTANCE.
ME?
I'D LOVE TO HELP.
THEN YOU MUST CEASE THE PLAGUED THINKING THAT HAS INFECTED THE WORLD OUT THERE, MISTER REECE.
THINK LESS OF HOW IT ENDS...AND CONSIDER HOW IT ALL BEGAN.

NECROPOLIS.
THANOS IS NOT PLEASED, PROXIMA...
HE FINDS THAT VARIABLES CHAFE, AND THIS LATEST ONE--A MOST COARSE KERNEL OF ENLIGHTENMENT.
THANOS FINDS ALL OF LIVING AN IRRITANT, CORVUS...FORGIVE ME IF I DON'T LEAP BEFORE SO ORDERED.
THIS IS DIFFERENT. THIS... CHANGE AT THE INCURSION POINTS.
WE'VE KILLED, WHAT, DOZENS OF WORLDS BY NOW?
FOURTEEN, HUSBAND. FOURTEEN RIGHTEOUS AND GLORIOUS ANNIHILATIONS.
AND EACH TIME, AS SOON AS THE WORLD IS GONE, THE INCURSION POINT COLLAPSES.
BUT NOW, ACCORDING TO OUR MASTER, IT LINGERS-- NOT LONG, BUT ENOUGH FOR THANOS TO CATALOG.
SO?
THAT PERIOD OF TIME IS EXPANDING. THANOS BELIEVES THAT--
HOLD.

WHAT...?
I THOUGHT... I WAS CERTAIN THAT...THERE WAS SOMEONE...
AND APPARENTLY I WAS WRONG.
JUMPY. LIKE A HURR IN WATER.
HRMPT.
SO... EXPANSION.
YES. THANOS SAYS THE CONCERN IS FOUND IN THE CONNECTIVE TISSUE--WHAT LINGERS SHOULD NOT EXIST--AND THEN HE BEGINS TO RAMBLE ON ABOUT BUBBLES OF OTHER...
"DESPAIR..."

DESPAIR LEADS TO DESPERATION-- A LAND THAT NO MAN SHOULD LONG TO VISIT--BUT FOR *YOU*, STARK...
FOR YOU THERE IS WHERE HOPE CAN BE FOUND. BECAUSE YOU CAN STILL BE USEFUL. YOU CAN STILL HELP SHAPE THE VERY END OF THINGS. YOU CAN--
DAY AFTER DAY.
I'VE BEEN HERE FOR MONTHS NOW. SITTING IN THIS BOX, HOUR BLEEDING INTO HOUR.
THEY SAY THAT ISOLATION IS THE SUREST PATH TO MADNESS, BUT I'VE FOUND IT... ILLUMINATING.
I HAVE FOUND A CONSTANT THAT NEVER FAILS.
YOU.
EVERY DAY--DAY AFTER DAY--YOU SHOW UP. OFFERING ME A WAY OUT. OFFERING ME YOUR LATEST FLAVOR OF SALVATION.
I USED TO THINK IT HAD TO DO WITH ME BEING A GENERALLY USEFUL GUY--A BUILDER--BUT YOU KNOW WHAT I THINK NOW?
WHAT?

I THINK YOU'RE IN LOVE.
DON'T BE OFFENDED--I THINK YOU'VE BEEN LOOKING FOR A WAY OUT FOR A VERY LONG TIME, AND NOW THAT WE'RE FINALLY GETTING DOWN TO IT...I JUST MIGHT BE YOUR LAST, BEST HOPE.
IT REALLY COMES DOWN TO THE SCIENCE OF ATTRACTION WITHIN CLEARLY DEFINED LIMITS. YOU'RE BOUND BY EVER-REDUCING OPTIONS AND PROXIMITY, KIDDO...
PLUS... LOOK AT THIS FACE.
I'M NOT LOOKING FOR A WAY OUT, ANTHONY. AS I HAVE TOLD YOU FROM THE VERY FIRST TIME I MET ANY OF YOU: THERE IS NO OUT.
THERE IS NO ESCAPING THIS.
I'LL CONCEDE, YOU PUT ON A GOOD SHOW...BUT THE PROBLEM IS I KNOW IT'S AN *ACT*. SEE, REED TOLD ME WHAT YOU'RE HIDING INSIDE OF YOU.
YOUR LITTLE SECRET.

"EXTENSIVE D.N.A. SAMPLES--FULL MEDICALS AND BRAIN SCANS, INCLUDING COGNITIVE MAPPING."
YOU'RE JUMPING FROM WORLD TO WORLD, LOOKING FOR A REFUGE SO YOU CAN REGROW YOUR LOVED ONES AND GET YOUR FAMILY BACK.
YOU'RE NOT A BLACK SWAN AT ALL...
YOU JUST PRESENT AS ONE.
AND WHO ARE YOU BUT WHAT THE WHEEL HAS MADE YOU?
A GOOD MAN? I THINK NOT.
LOOK AT WHAT YOU BECAME. LOOK AT THE THINGS YOU MADE.
LOOK AT WHERE YOU ARE.
YOU FORGET... I WAS THERE THE LAST TIME YOU TRIED TO BE A HERO.

"WHEN YOU TRIED
TO SAVE THE
LIVES OF THOSE
ALREADY LOST.
"I WATCHED
YOU FALL."

AND THEN THEY PUT YOU HERE...IN THIS CAGE.
JUST SO YOU KNOW...
...NOTHING YOU'RE SAYING MAKES WHAT I SAID UNTRUE.
I SUPPOSE NOT.
BUT I WILL FIND WHAT I AM SEARCHING FOR, STARK...AND WHEN THAT HAPPENS, YOU'LL STILL BE HERE...
ROTTING AWAY.
REGRETTING WHAT A FOOL YOU ARE, AND WHAT FOOLISH THINGS YOU SAID.
GOODBYE...
I WILL NOT BE RETURNING.

WELL, I'LL BE DAMNED...

JESSICA. NATASHA.
AREN'T THE TWO OF YOU A SIGHT FOR SORE EYES.
ALTHOUGH...
I SUPPOSE IT MIGHT ACTUALLY BE CAUSE FOR **ALARM**. ARE YOU HERE ON BEHALF OF MY FRIENDS WHO WANT NOTHING TO DO WITH ME?
OR ON BEHALF OF MY FRIENDS WHO WANT TO **KILL** ME?
OH, ANTHONY...
IT'S AMAZING THAT YOU STILL THINK YOU HAVE FRIENDS AT ALL.
AND WE'RE HERE ON OUR OWN.
NO ONE ELSE KNOWS WHERE YOU ARE.
IF THAT'S THE CASE...THEN HOW DID YOU FIND ME?
STEVE. IT WAS LATE ONE NIGHT. WE WERE TALKING. NORMALLY... WELL, LATELY, ALL HE DOES IS PLAN. ALL HE DOES IS CHASE.
MOST PEOPLE HAVEN'T REALIZED-- THEY DON'T KNOW WHAT TO LOOK FOR, THEY JUST SEE HOW STRONG HE IS-- BUT...ALL THIS...
IT'S TAKEN ITS TOLL.
WELL... WE'VE **ALL** SUFFERED, HAVEN'T WE?

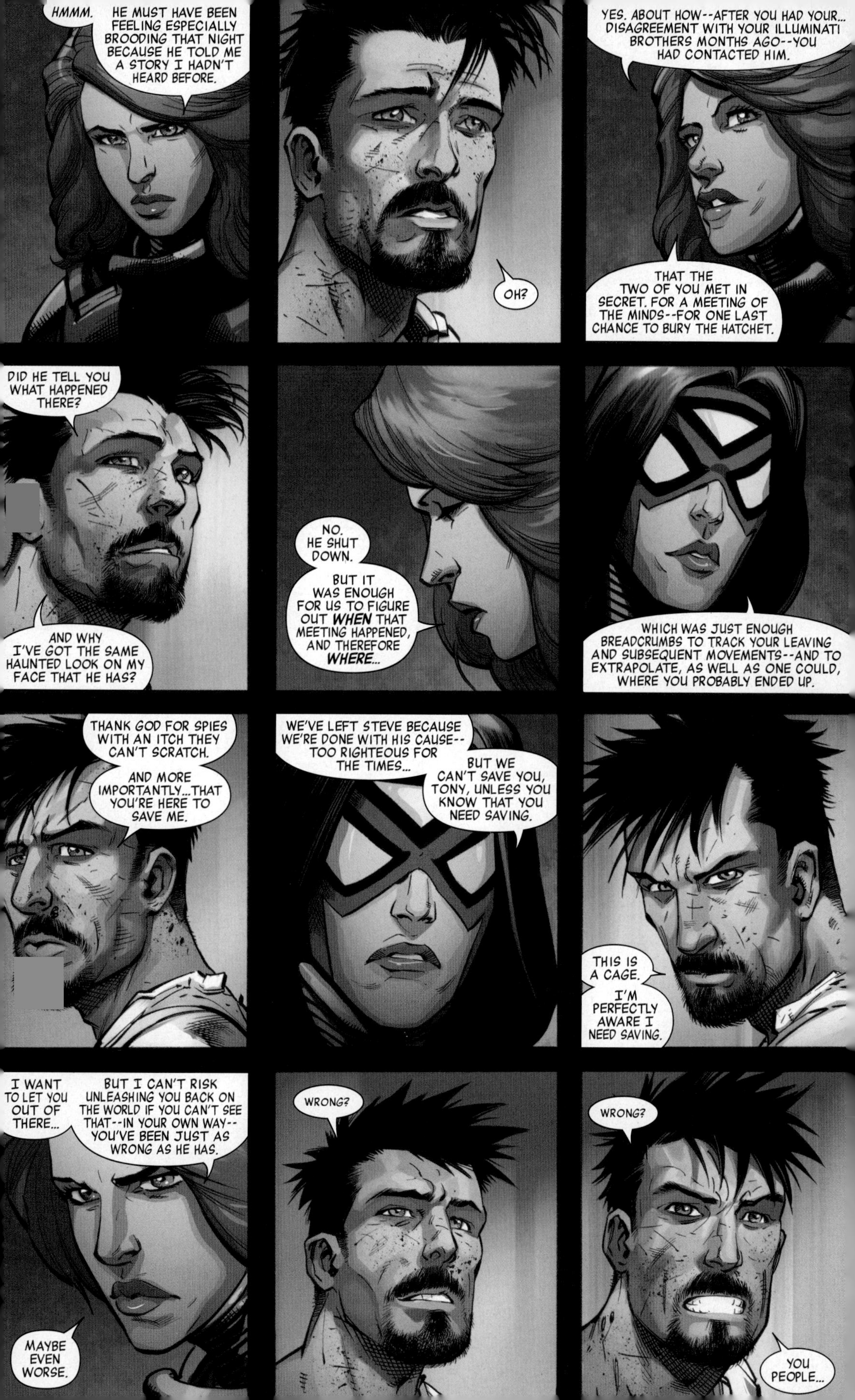
HMMM.
HE MUST HAVE BEEN FEELING ESPECIALLY BROODING THAT NIGHT BECAUSE HE TOLD ME A STORY I HADN'T HEARD BEFORE.
OH?
YES. ABOUT HOW--AFTER YOU HAD YOUR... DISAGREEMENT WITH YOUR ILLUMINATI BROTHERS MONTHS AGO--YOU HAD CONTACTED HIM.
THAT THE TWO OF YOU MET IN SECRET. FOR A MEETING OF THE MINDS--FOR ONE LAST CHANCE TO BURY THE HATCHET.
DID HE TELL YOU WHAT HAPPENED THERE?
AND WHY I'VE GOT THE SAME HAUNTED LOOK ON MY FACE THAT HE HAS?
NO. HE SHUT DOWN.
BUT IT WAS ENOUGH FOR US TO FIGURE OUT **WHEN** THAT MEETING HAPPENED, AND THEREFORE **WHERE**...
WHICH WAS JUST ENOUGH BREADCRUMBS TO TRACK YOUR LEAVING AND SUBSEQUENT MOVEMENTS--AND TO EXTRAPOLATE, AS WELL AS ONE COULD, WHERE YOU PROBABLY ENDED UP.
THANK GOD FOR SPIES WITH AN ITCH THEY CAN'T SCRATCH.
AND MORE IMPORTANTLY...THAT YOU'RE HERE TO SAVE ME.
WE'VE LEFT STEVE BECAUSE WE'RE DONE WITH HIS CAUSE--TOO RIGHTEOUS FOR THE TIMES...
BUT WE CAN'T SAVE YOU, TONY, UNLESS YOU KNOW THAT YOU NEED SAVING.
THIS IS A CAGE.
I'M PERFECTLY AWARE I NEED SAVING.
I WANT TO LET YOU OUT OF THERE...
BUT I CAN'T RISK UNLEASHING YOU BACK ON THE WORLD IF YOU CAN'T SEE THAT--IN YOUR OWN WAY--YOU'VE BEEN JUST AS WRONG AS HE HAS.
MAYBE EVEN WORSE.
WRONG?
WRONG?
YOU PEOPLE...

WRONG?
I HAVEN'T BEEN WRONG ONCE!
THERE'S NOT A SINGLE DECISION I'VE MADE THAT I WOULD CHANGE.
UNLEASH ME? UNLEASH ME?
YOU SHOULD THANK WHATEVER GOD YOU WORSHIP THAT I'M ALIVE TO SAVE YOU.
GREAT! WALK AWAY!
IT DOESN'T MATTER. YOU'LL BE BACK.
BUT MAKE SURE WHEN YOU DO COME BACK--BECAUSE YOU NEED ME--THAT IT'S ON YOUR KNEES.
BOTH OF YOU! REPENTANT!
BECAUSE I CAN'T SAVE ANY OF YOU, UNLESS YOU REALIZE THAT YOU NEED SAVING!
AND THAT I'M THE ONLY ONE ON THIS ENTIRE PLANET WHO CAN DO IT!

"ORIGIN SITES"

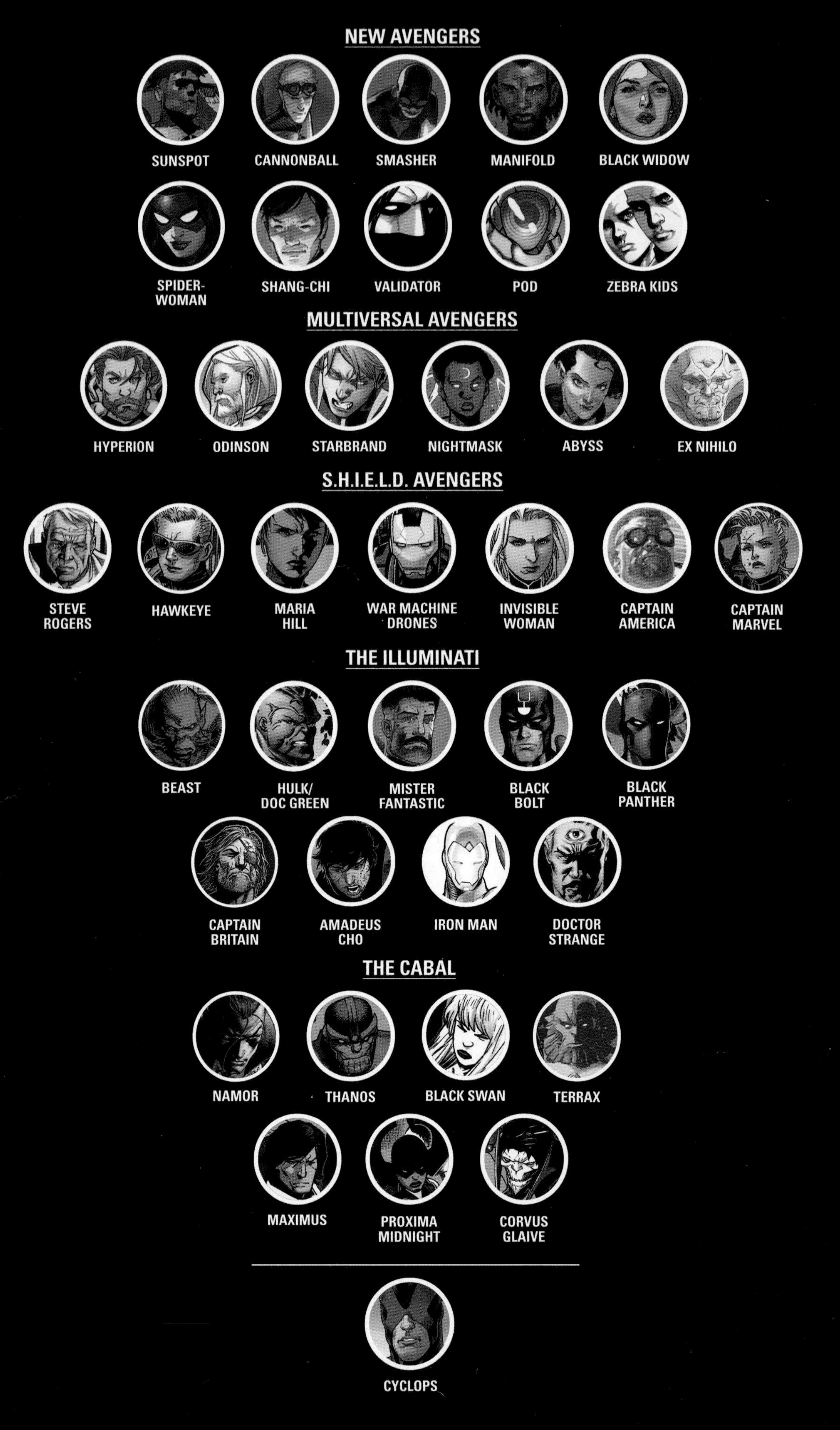
NEW AVENGERS
SUNSPOT
CANNONBALL
SMASHER
MANIFOLD
BLACK WIDOW
SPIDER-WOMAN
SHANG-CHI
VALIDATOR
POD
ZEBRA KIDS
MULTIVERSAL AVENGERS
HYPERION
ODINSON
STARBRAND
NIGHTMASK
ABYSS
EX NIHILO
S.H.I.E.L.D. AVENGERS
STEVE ROGERS
HAWKEYE
MARIA HILL
WAR MACHINE DRONES
INVISIBLE WOMAN
CAPTAIN AMERICA
CAPTAIN MARVEL
THE ILLUMINATI
BEAST
HULK/ DOC GREEN
MISTER FANTASTIC
BLACK BOLT
BLACK PANTHER
CAPTAIN BRITAIN
AMADEUS CHO
IRON MAN
DOCTOR STRANGE
THE CABAL
NAMOR
THANOS
BLACK SWAN
TERRAX
MAXIMUS
PROXIMA MIDNIGHT
CORVUS GLAIVE
CYCLOPS

PREVIOUSLY IN AVENGERS

KOBE, JAPAN.
QUARANTINED ORIGIN BOMB SITE.
ONE DAY AGO.
SYSTEM QUERY: USER?
SYSTEM STATUS: USER: ONLINE.
SYSTEM QUERY: USER STATUS?
USER STATUS: I LIKE KITTY CATS.
MEORR.
THAT'S NOT A KITTY CAT.

I, THE SYSTEM, COME ONLINE IN THE DISTANCE BETWEEN THE RED [NOW GREEN] DOT AND THE BLUE.
BETWEEN THE ORIGIN OF THE PURPOSE AND ITS EXECUTION.
THE SYSTEM IS PERFECT.
I AM PERFECT: A WEAPON.
I BECOME WE. THE FIRE FROZEN. THE COLD A PERFECT CHRYSALIS FOR THE PLANETARY DYNAMO.
AN OUTER SHELL OUR FIRST ARMOR. SOFT COMPARED TO WHAT THE SYSTEM IS FORMING.

A PROTECTIVE VOID FOR THE WE TO LEARN. TO JOIN. TO TRAIN. TO GROW.
THE SYSTEM IS A PART OF A LARGER SYSTEM.
THE LARGER SYSTEM IN PERIL.
THE WE SYSTEM [IN SERVICE TO THE GREATER SYSTEM] PARTIALLY COMES ONLINE.

THE I PROTECTS
THE USER PROTECTS
THE WE PROTECTS
THE GREATER SYSTEM.
THE WEAPON FULLY FUNCTIONAL [UPGRADE. UPGRADE. UPGRADE.]
THE WE PARTIALLY FUNCTIONAL [CONFUSED. AFRAID. PANIC.]
THE GREATER SYSTEM FAILS. THE WE SYSTEM REMOVED FROM THE OTHER SYSTEMS.
ADRIFT.
LOST.

WE.
WE BECOME WE.
WE LEARN. THE WEAPON IS FULLY FUNCTIONAL. THE SYSTEM IS FULLY FUNCTIONAL. THE WE IS FULLY FUNCTIONAL.
WE WAIT...
AND THEN WE HEAR A VOICE. IT SAYS...
WELCO BACK.

THE SAVAGE LAND.
NOW.
OKAY... LET'S GET STARTED.
SOME OF YOU KNOW ONE ANOTHER, SOME DON'T...BUT WE'LL SAVE THE INTRODUCTORY BITS FOR LATER.

FIRST--WHILE SOME OF YOU HAVE BEEN WORKING WITH ME FOR MONTHS NOW, THE REST ARE COMING INTO THIS A LITTLE BEHIND THE CURVE.
YOU'RE GOING TO WANT TO FOCUS ON THE "WHY" HERE, AS IT'S THE MOST IMPORTANT THING.
PROBABLY THE *ONLY* THING.
NEXT SCREEN, ZEBRAS.
SO HERE WE GO:
MONTHS AGO, A.I.M. THEORETICIANS DISCOVERED THAT THE MULTIVERSE--ALL EXISTING UNIVERSES--WERE IN AN UNNATURAL STATE OF DECAY.
A TERMINAL ONE.
THIS WILL NOT COME AS A SURPRISE TO YOU AS, WELL, BASICALLY EVERYONE ON THE PLANET KNOWS THIS NOW.
YOU'RE ALSO AWARE THAT THERE HAVE BEEN OTHER GROUPS ACTIVELY WORKING TO, AT WORST, ABATE AND, AT BEST, SOLVE THIS VERY PROBLEM.
SOLVE?
I'M STILL CATCHING UP, BUT THAT SEEMS GENEROUS, DOESN'T IT, BOBBY?

MAYBE IF YOU WANT TO ARGUE EFFECTIVENESS, BUT IF YOU WANT TO ARGUE INTENT? I DUNNO...I GREW UP IDOLIZING SOME OF THESE GUYS. IT MIGHT BE A SHORTCOMING, BUT I STILL GIVE THEM THE BENEFIT OF THE DOUBT.
WHAT I DO KNOW IS THAT THE ILLUMINATI HAD A PLAN TO GET AT THE HEART OF ALL THIS, INCLUDING SENDING SOMEONE OUT THERE--INTO THE MULTIVERSE--TO FIND OUT WHO CAUSED THIS.
WHICH IS WHY, WORKING TOGETHER WITH THE INDIGENOUS ENGINEERS HERE IN THE SAVAGE LAND--
THANK YOU.
YOU'RE WELCOME.
--A.I.M. SCIENTISTS REDESIGNED AND BUILT AN AUGER STRONG ENOUGH TO PROJECT AN ASSAULT TEAM ACROSS THE MULTIVERSE TO ALSO TRY TO FIND OUT WHOEVER IS BEHIND THE COLLAPSE...
AND MAYBE EVEN STOP IT BY, YOU KNOW...PUNCHING THE PROBLEM TO DEATH.
LIKE AVENGERS.
WAIT. HOW DO YOU KNOW THAT?
I DUNNO. MAYBE IT'S A GENERAL MOOD I'M SENSING? I MEAN, THOR DOESN'T HAVE HIS HAMMER ANYMORE, BUT MY GOD, IZZY...THE LOOK IN THE GUY'S EYES IS ENOUGH FOR ME TO--
NO. THAT'S NOT WHAT I MEANT.
HOW DO YOU KNOW THAT THE ILLUMINATI SENT SOMEONE?
OH. THAT.
WELL...WE'VE HAD SOMEONE INSIDE THEIR OPERATION FOR THE LAST MONTH.

NATION X. TWO DAYS AGO.
HE ASKED FOR MY HELP, SO I WAS, IN SPITE OF OLD WOUNDS, HAPPY TO GIVE IT...
BUT THERE ARE RULES, ROBERTO. I... HAVE RULES.
THIS PLACE IS A HAVEN FOR ANYONE WHO CALLS THEMSELVES MUTANT, AND WE STAND IN OPPOSITION TO ANYONE WHO WOULD MEAN OUR KIND HARM...
BUT I WILL NOT ACCEPT BEING SWEPT UP IN WHATEVER IT IS HE IS PLANNING HERE TODAY.
WE HAVE OUR OWN...IDEAS ABOUT HOW TO STOP WHAT'S HAPPENING, AND HAVE NO TIME FOR DISTRACTIONS. UNDERSTAND?
UH-HUH. DON'T CRAP ON THE LAWN. GOT IT.
MAN...LOOK AT THIS STUFF. THESE THINGS USED TO CREEP ME OUT.
YES. AND NOW THEY MAKE A GOOD WARNING:
ABANDON HATE ALL YE WHO ENTER HERE.
WELL, IT'S CERTAINLY A MESSAGE. I'LL GIVE YOU THAT.
SO WHAT'S YOUR PLAN?
HMM?
"WE HAVE OUR OWN...IDEAS ABOUT HOW TO STOP WHAT'S HAPPENING"...
BECAUSE, CYCLOPS, IF YOU'VE TRULY GOT SOMETHING-- I THINK WE'RE ROUNDING INTO THE PERFECT OPPORTUNITY FOR YOU TO GENERATE SOME OF THAT LIFELONG GLOBAL GOOD WILL YOU'VE CRAVED YOUR ENTIRE LIFE.
IF I'M BEING HONEST...ALL IT MAKES ME THINK ABOUT IS STARTING A FIRE.
WHAT DO YOU MEAN, SCOTT?
THIS ISN'T THE FUTURE WE DESERVED, IS IT?
BUT THEN AGAIN, IT NEVER IS. THAT'S WHY YOU DON'T LET THE WORLD SHAPE YOU--YOU SHAPE IT. JUST LIKE PROFESSOR X TAUGHT US.
YOU DO IT AS BEST YOU CAN.

I HAVE A PHOENIX EGG, ROBERTO.
AND I THINK IT'S PAST TIME I GOT IN THE GAME.
YOU CAN'T BE THINKING OF--
OF COURSE I AM.
BUT HERE'S YOUR GUY NOW. WE'LL TALK LATER.
ROBERTO.
SCOTT.
HANK.
THAT IS A VERY DANGEROUS MAN, DOCTOR McCOY.
YES. A MAN OF THE TIMES, ONE MIGHT SAY.
SO HOW CAN I HELP YOU, HANK? WHAT'S ALL THIS ABOUT?
CONFESSION. ABSOLUTION.
YOUNG MAN... I AM LOST AND IN GREAT NEED OF RESCUE.
I NEED YOUR HELP.

AND THEN, AFTER HE FILLED ME IN ON ALL THE VARIOUS MACHINATIONS WE WERE IGNORANT OF... HE BASICALLY TOLD ME EVERYTHING THE ILLUMINATI WERE UP TO.
INCLUDING THE FACT THAT THEY HAVE A PLAN FOR BOTH SETTLING UP WITH THE S.H.I.E.L.D. TEAM AND ELIMINATING THE CABAL FROM THE EQUATION.

AND HE TOLD ME THEY WERE GOING TO DO IT SOON.

CAN I JUST SAY...
I HONESTLY HAVE NO IDEA WHO I'M SUPPOSED TO BE SUPPORTING HERE.
WE ALL LEFT THE AVENGERS BECAUSE WE REFUSED TO HUNT "OTHER AVENGERS"--BUT THEN WE ALSO COMPLETELY WASHED OUR HANDS OF THE ILLUMINATI BECAUSE OF WHAT THEY WERE DOING...
SO, I'M *LOST*, MAN.

THAT'S THE POINT, EDEN.
SO ARE *THEY*. ALL OF THEM.

THAT'S WHY WE HAVE TO STOP THEM FROM FIGHTING EACH OTHER AND FIND SOME WAY TO REMIND THEM OF WHO THEY ARE...
AND WHAT THEY'RE SUPPOSED TO *BE*.
THAT'S OUR MISSION. OUR GOAL.

OKAY.
WELL, IF THE ILLUMINATI ARE SETTING A TRAP, THEN WHY DON'T WE JUST--
PROBLEM IS... THEY'RE NOT THE ONLY ONES RUNNING A CON.
SO IS S.H.I.E.L.D.
AND HOW DO YOU KNOW *THAT?*
YOU REALLY SHOULD HAVE BEEN ABLE TO FIGURE THAT ONE OUT BY WHO'S IN THE ROOM.
SYSTEM LOADED
I WAS OFF-PLANET FOR A WHILE.
WELL... WELCOME HOME, EARTHMAN.

THE SAVAGE LAND.
THREE DAYS AGO.
SO NO ONE KNOWS YOU'RE HERE?
WE SLIPPED ALL OUR SURVEILLANCE BEFORE WE CROSSED INTO MEXICO.
IT TOOK A LITTLE TIME...BUT GETTING HERE INCOGNITO WASN'T THAT DIFFICULT, ROBERTO.
WE'RE PRETTY GOOD AT THIS.
AND THEN YOU CAME STRAIGHT HERE?
YES.

OKAY. WE'RE GOING TO NEED TO HANDLE THIS THE RIGHT WAY...
HOLD ON A SECOND. HOW IS IT THAT NEITHER ONE OF YOU CAN TELL WHEN A WOMAN IS LYING TO YOU?
THEY'RE *LYING* TO YOU.
I LIKE TO THINK I'M NON-JUDGMENTAL AND BELIEVE THAT MOST PEOPLE, WHEN GIVEN THE CHANCE, PREFER TO TELL THE TRUTH.
AND I'M TOTALLY SELF-ABSORBED.
HONESTLY, I'M NOT EVEN LISTENING WHEN MOST PEOPLE ARE TALKING.
EVEN ME?
REALLY?
WHAT?
I THINK I'M GOING TO HAVE STEAK FOR DINNER.
YOU DIDN'T COME STRAIGHT HERE, DID YOU?
NO.
WE THOUGHT SOMEONE NEEDED OUR HELP...
WE WERE WRONG--WE'RE HERE NOW.
AND SOMETHING HAS TO BE DONE ABOUT S.H.I.E.L.D.

STEVE ROGERS HAS ASSUMED THAT HIS...ENEMY IS SMARTER THAN HIM. SO HIS ONLY RECOURSE WAS REDUNDANCY AND OVERWHELMING FORCE...
TO THAT END, HE HAS QUIETLY ASSEMBLED SECONDARY AND TERTIARY TEAMS THAT ALMOST NO ONE KNOWS ABOUT.
THE ILLUMINATI THINK THEIR ADVERSARY IS ONE THING, WHEN IN FACT IT IS SOMETHING ELSE ALTOGETHER.
AND WITH THAT...YOU KNOW EVERYTHING.
IT'S ALL LAID OUT ON THE TABLE.
WE HAVE TO OVERCOME THESE THINGS, AND AT THE SAME TIME CONVINCE OUR FRIENDS--WHO HAVE LOST THEIR WAY--TO REDISCOVER COMMON GROUND FOR THE COMMON GOOD.
SO NO BIG DEAL, RIGHT?
JUST WIN AGAINST A GROUP OF SUPER-INTELLECTS WHO SEE THINGS FIVE MOVES AHEAD AT THE SAME TIME WE'RE FACING SOME KIND OF AVENGERS ARMY COBBLED TOGETHER BY AMERICA'S SUPER-ANGRY GREATEST WARTIME HERO...
SURE. AND THEN WE'LL ALL HAVE PIE.
YOU DO ACTUALLY HAVE SOMETHING UP YOUR SLEEVE, RIGHT?
BECAUSE ALL THIS BLUSTER LEADING TO NOTHING...
NOT A GOOD LOOK.
ACTUALLY, I DO HAVE THE SMARTEST EX-EVIL SCIENTISTS CURRENTLY BUILDING SOME VERY IMPRESSIVE MACHINES, BUT US--WE HERE IN THIS ROOM--ARE ENOUGH.
DO YOU REMEMBER HOW ALL THIS STARTED? EX NIHILO AND HIS ORIGIN BOMBS? HE WANTED TO REMAKE THE EARTH, BUT DO YOU KNOW WHAT HE REALLY DID?
HE KICKSTARTED OUR AVENGERS WORLD.

I WAS AIKKU JOKINEN.
NO, I *AM* AIKKU JOKINEN.
MY PARENTS ARE FINNISH, BUT I WAS BORN IN NORWAY, THEIR ONLY CHILD.
I DON'T LIKE THE COLD, BUT LOVE THE OUTDOORS. I LOVE CHOCOLATE AND MY GIRLFRIEND, DARJA. I LOVE ALL THE THINGS I ALWAYS HAVE...
AR
WHEN I FIRST WOKE, I DID NOT UNDERSTAND WHAT HAD HAPPENED.
I AM STILL AIKKU, BUT ALSO...WE.
[CONFUSED. AFRAID. PANIC.]

THEN I HEARD
THE WEAPON.
IT SPOKE TO ME.

IT SPOKE...
INSIDE ME.

WE.
I LEARNED WHAT
I NOW WAS.
WE LEARNED.

WE.
WE ARE A
WEAPON.

SEVEN SITES.
STARBRAND ACCIDENTLY DESTROYED THE EARTHMIND--THE SELF-AWARENESS SITE. AND WE WERE FORCED TO ELIMINATE BOTH THE SELF-REPAIR AND COMMUNICATION NODES.
BUT FOUR REMAINED ACTIVE. HEALTHY AND VIBRANT... AN AVENGERS WORLD.
AND WE HAVE ALL THE POWER WE NEED. SELF-SUSTENANCE CONTROLLED BY THE ZEBRAS.
WE HAVE THE WORLD'S MOST POWERFUL SELF-DEFENSE MECHANISM: POD.
WE CONTROL THE POWER OF EVOLUTION: VALIDATOR.
AND WE HAVE AN ARMY THANKS TO THE FINAL SITE...

"WHEN SHANG-CHI OFFERED TO EXPLORE THE KOBE SITE MONTHS AGO, IT WAS BEFORE WE HAD RECOVERED POD AND REALLY BEGAN TO UNDERSTAND WHAT WAS AT WORK.
"WE DIDN'T FULLY KNOW WHAT EACH SITE'S PURPOSE WAS. AND NOW WE DO.
"IT TOOK HIM MONTHS, BUT SHANG FINALLY FIGURED OUT HOW TO... COMMUNE WITH THE MALLEABLE GENESIS MATTER THAT WAS BOTH THE BY-PRODUCT AND THE COLLECTIVE SENTIENT REMAINS OF THE PEOPLE WHO ONCE LIVED THERE.
"THEY WERE BASICALLY WAITING TO BE REMADE. REBORN. WHATEVER.
"BOTH THE HAND AND TWO S.H.I.E.L.D. TEAMS HAVE DISAPPEARED IN THE KOBE ZONE--SHANG BELIEVES THEY TRIED TO RESIST THE GENESIS MATTER."
"IT ABSORBED THEM AS WELL. SO SHANG WENT THE OTHER WAY AND SUBMITTED..."
"AND BY DOING THAT, GAINED CONTROL OF THE SITE AND THE POWER IT WIELDED.
"IT WAS THE POWER OF REPLICATION...

"AND NOW A MAN HAS BECOME AN ARMY."

MULTIVERSAL AVENGERS
HYPERION
ODINSON
STARBRAND
NIGHTMASK
ABYSS
EX NIHILO
NEW AVENGERS
SUNSPOT
CANNONBALL
SMASHER
MANIFOLD
BLACK WIDOW
SPIDER-WOMAN
SHANG-CHI
VALIDATOR
POD
ZEBRA KIDS
S.H.I.E.L.D. AVENGERS
STEVE ROGERS
HAWKEYE
MARIA HILL
WAR MACHINE DRONES
INVISIBLE WOMAN
CAPTAIN AMERICA
CAPTAIN MARVEL
THE ILLUMINATI
BEAST
HULK/ DOC GREEN
MISTER FANTASTIC
BLACK BOLT
BLACK PANTHER
CAPTAIN BRITAIN
AMADEUS CHO
IRON MAN
DOCTOR STRANGE
THE CABAL
NAMOR
THANOS
BLACK SWAN
TERRAX
MAXIMUS
PROXIMA MIDNIGHT
CORVUS GLAIVE
DOCTOR DOOM
THE MAD THINKER
MOLECULE MAN

THE NOTHING SPACE OF DESTROYED UNIVERSES.
THE TEMPLE OF THE BLACK PRIESTS.
SOMETHIIIIIING SHIIIIIIMERS...
SOMETHIIIIIING SPARKS...
COMPANY'S HERE.

FFWASHHHHHH!
FOUND IT!
SEE...I TOLD YOU IT WAS OUT HERE, BUT WHICH ONES ARE THES--
BLACK PRIESTS!
THEY KILL WITH A WORD...
"QUICKLY! BEFORE THEY CAN SPEAK THEM!"
LIFE, EXISTING IN A PLACE WHERE IT SHOULDN'T...

"...NOT A MIRACLE, BUT A MALFORMATION."
LIIIIIFE GENERATIIIIING SYSTEMS OF THE BUIIIIILDERS...
DEFENSELESS TO RIIIIGHT WORD.
SPEAK THE WORD, PRIIIIESTS. SPEAK THE WORD.
NO!

THE OTHER SIDE IS COLLAPSING, ABYSS--YOU CAN RELEASE THE GATE.
WE WON'T BE LEAVING THE WAY WE CAME.
WHERE ARE WE?
NOT SURE, HYPERION, BUT WHEREVER IT IS, WE'VE FOUND THE BLACK PRIESTS. WE SHOULD HAVE HAD SURPRISE ON OUR SIDE--BUT THE PRIESTS HAVE ALREADY BEGUN RESPONDING.
WE ARE LOSING NIHILII.
GODS.
I'M COUNTING THOUSANDS. MAYBE MORE...
"SINCE THE AUGER, WE'VE BEEN DROWNING IN SIDERA MARIS--OUR ONLY ENCOUNTER WITH THE PRIESTS WAS THE ONE WE DEFEATED SEVERAL JUMPS AGO...
"BUT THIS MUST BE THEIR SEAT OF POWER--WE'RE VASTLY OUTNUMBERED WITH NOWHERE TO GO!"
WHEN, IN THESE LAST DAYS, HAVE WE NOT FACED THE UNSPEAKABLE.

THE TIMES, THEY TRY TO SHAPE US.
PERHAPS INSTEAD OF FIGHTING IT...
...WE SHOULD EMBRACE IT.
"WHOSOEVER HOLDS THIS HAMMER, IF HE BE UNWORTHY, SHALL POSSESS THE POWER OF THORR."
ONCE, I WAS WORTHY. NOW, IT IS NO LONGER SO.
THERE WAS A TIME WHEN I KNEW THAT I WOULD MEET MY FATE IN BATTLE, WITH MJOLNIR IN HAND.
I STILL BELIEVE THAT TO BE TRUE.

IF THIS IS OUR FATE, SO BE IT.
BUT IF I AM TO DIE, LET IT BE WITH LIGHTNING AND THUNDER...
...AND THE POWER OF THORR.

THOR, WHY ARE YOU LAUGHING? IS THIS SUPPOSED TO BE FUN?
GODS! YES!
GOOD TO HAVE YOU BACK, BROTHER.
THOOOOMM!
GOOD TO BE BACK.

ARGGGH!
OH! I GET IT NOW--HOW THE WORDS WORK! IT'S REALITY DISPLACEMENT. THEY'RE ATTACKING THE TANGIBLE WORLD WITH LANGUAGE. UNDERSTAND?
I DO. THEY'RE MANIPULATING THE BASE CODE OF EVERYTHING--REORDERING THE SEQUENCING OF MATTER.
YOU HAVE TO STOP THEM FROM BUILDING THE WORDS.
YOU DON'T HAVE TO DEFEAT ALL OF THEM--JUST STOP THEM FROM COMING TOGETHER!
KRAK-A-THOOM!

IT WORKED!
YES! QUICKLY NOW... PRESS THE ADVANTAGE.
THE WORDS. THE WORDS ARE LOST.
ALL IIIIIIIIS LOST IF WE HAVE LOST THE WORDS.
WAIIIIIT. WAIIIIIT.
THE EYE.
THE EYE...

HE COMES.
WHO'S THIS?
IT DOESN'T MATTER--OUR STRATEGY IS WORKING.
JUST PREVENT HIM FROM COMBINING WITH THE OTHERS.
I CANNOT MOVE.
ME NEITHER.
HOW DID IT DO THAT?

HOW?
AS WITH ALL THINGS, WITH PRACTICE AND EXPERIENCE.
WHICH IS ANOTHER WORD FOR EXPERTISE.
OF WHICH I HAVE AN ABUNDANCE.
AH! IT HAS BEEN SOME TIME, ODINSON.
STEPHEN?
WELCOME, MY OLD FRIEND...
WELCOME TO MY SANCTUM.

LATVERIA.
THE RABBLE LOVE STORIES.
THEY LOVE THE LIE, WHICH IS WHY THERE IS NO DISCERNIBLE DIFFERENCE BETWEEN WHAT THEY CALL TRUTH AND WHAT THEY CALL FICTION.
HISTORY. A COLLECTION OF HALF-TRUTHS WEAVED TOGETHER SO AS TO ESTABLISH A SUPPOSED FIRM FOUNDATION SUPPORTING ALL THAT HAS BEEN BUILT--MODERNITY.
WE CAN AGREE ON THIS, CAN'T WE, MISTER REECE?
LOTS OF CRACKS UNDERFOOT.
BEDROCK MADE OF AIR.
THEY THINK THEY UNDERSTAND WHO I AM--WHAT I AM--BUT THEY'RE WRONG. YOU'RE WRONG.
WHAT'S AN ORIGIN, BUT A STORY?
WHAT'S MY STORY, BUT A LIE?
WE ALL LOVE OUR STORIES, DON'T WE?

NO. FOR DOOM DOES NOT LIE.
NOT NOW. NOT EVER.
IF WHAT YOU THINK IS TRUE--AND YOU SAY IS TRUE--AND YOU BELIEVE IS TRUE--BUT IS IN FACT A WELL-CONSTRUCTED LIE...
THEN ARE YOU NOT A *LIAR?*
A LIAR FULL OF LIES. LIAR. FOOL. FOOL OF FOOLS. GOD OF FOOLS.
DOOM'S OPENING THE CONTAINER--BRING THE CONTAINMENT PROTOCOLS ONLINE.
REMEMBER TO WATCH FOR RESONANCE...
THE ONLY WAY WE WERE EVEN ABLE TO *FIND* THE MOLECULE MAN WAS BECAUSE HIS FREQUENCY PERFECTLY MATCHED THE MAPMAKER ARTIFACT.
TOO MUCH TALK. BUT IF WE *MUST* TALK, WE SHOULD TALK ABOUT BEGINNINGS--ALSO, ENDINGS...
DO YOU KNOW THE STORY? FIRST THERE WAS NOTHING... THEN THERE WAS EVERYTHING...
HEY. NICE ROCK.
YES. IT FELL FROM THE SKY.
A REMNANT OF A DESTROYED EARTH SET TO COLLIDE WITH OUR OWN. FROM IT WE HAVE...LEARNED THINGS. IT BROADCASTS A SIGNAL, ACTING AS A BUOY FOR WORLDS IN THE MULTIVERSE.
ENERGY SURGE!
STEADY. LEVELS ARE WITHIN TOLERANCE.

MAP. MAPS.
MAKING MAPS...
WE HAVE A PAN-UNIVERSAL PROBLEM, MISTER REECE, BUT I BELIEVE IT ORIGINATES *HERE.* ON EARTH.
EARTH? OH, IT'S HERE...
BUT IT'S *NOT* HERE.
I BELIEVE YOU.
I WANT YOU TO TELL ME A STORY, MISTER REECE--AND I WANT IT TO BE TRUE.
WHY DOES THE FREQUENCY OF THE ROCK'S SIGNAL MATCH YOUR OWN?
WHY IS ALL THIS HAPPENING? AND WHAT IS YOUR PART IN IT?
WHY?
WHY? WHY? WHY?
SHOW, DON'T TELL-- ACTIONS, NOT WORDS.
HEY, DOOM...

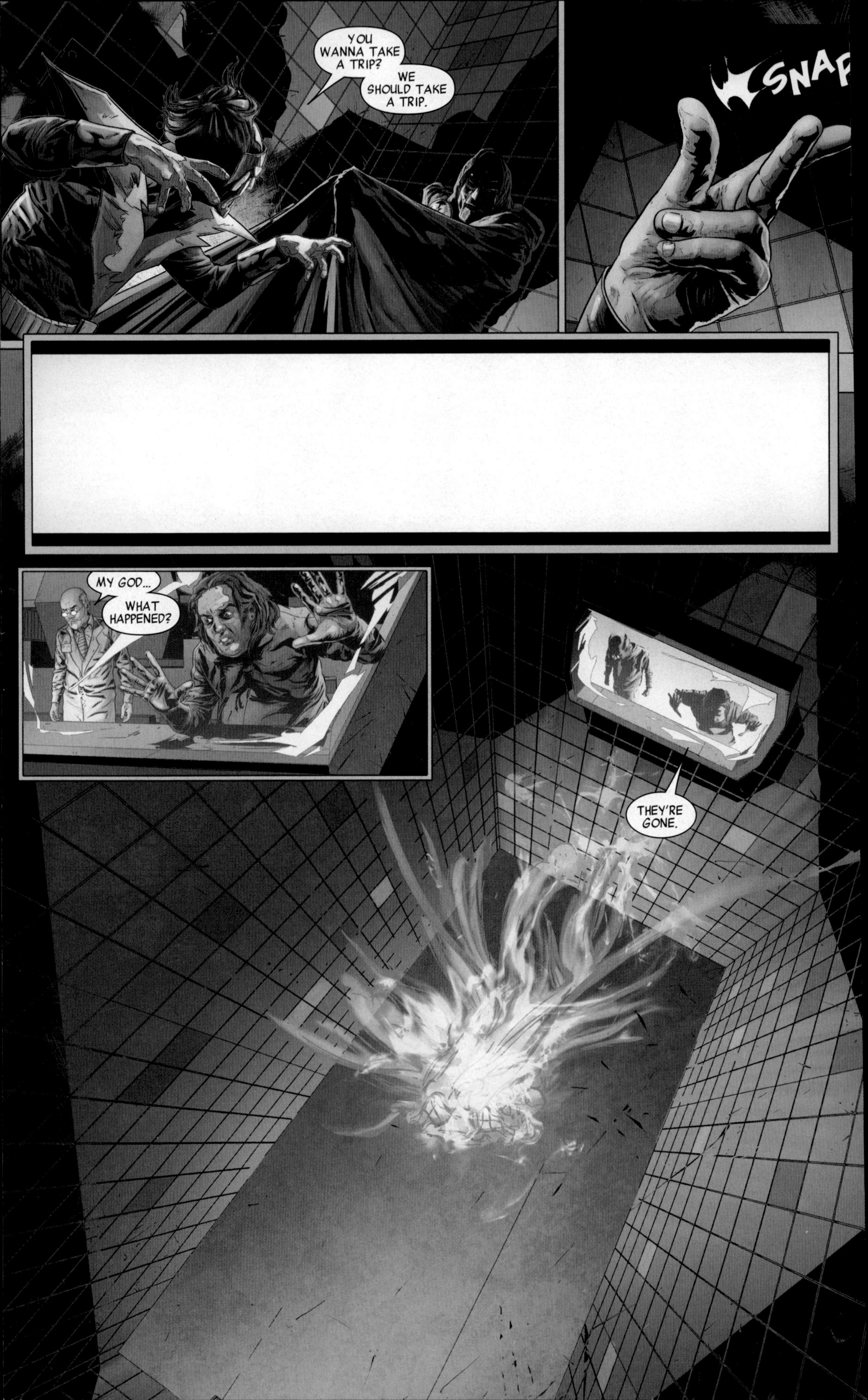

YOU WANNA TAKE A TRIP?
WE SHOULD TAKE A TRIP.
SNAP
MY GOD...
WHAT HAPPENED?
THEY'RE GONE.

I'M SURE
YOU HAVE QUESTIONS, ODINSON, AS DO I...THE EAST OF WHICH BEING WHAT HAPPENED TO YOUR ARM...
BUT DESPITE OUR QUICK RESOLUTION TO THE CONFLICT OUT THERE, THE PRIESTHOOD IS COLLECTIVELY CONCERNED ABOUT ONE EXCEEDINGLY IMPORTANT THING...
YES...
HOW DIIIID YOU FIIIIIND US OUT HERE IIIIIIN THE NOTHIIIIIING?
FLOATIIIING, CIIIIRCLIIIIING THE LOST SPACES?
WE DID.
WELL...HE DID. TELL THEM, NIGHTMASK.
I WAS MADE TO NAVIGATE THE SUPERFLOW--THE SPACE BETWEEN UNIVERSES.
I MINE THE IDEAS THAT USED TO EXIST THERE. WITH THE DESTRUCTION OF ENTIRE UNIVERSES, THE WEB-LIKE FLOWSPACE CAME UNDONE...LIKE COLLAPSING LATTICEWORK WITHOUT A FRAME.
BUT MY ABILITY TO FIND THINGS IN THE SPACES IN BETWEEN--THE ABILITY TO MINE BROADCASTED IDEAS--STILL FUNCTIONS. WE KNEW THAT SOME OF THE BEINGS ASSOCIATED WITH THE DESTRUCTION OF EVERYTHING EXISTED HERE.
SO FINDING YOU WAS EASY ONCE I STARTED LOOKING.
HE HEARD US? WAS HE LIIIISTENIIIING CLOSELY? DIIIIID HE HEAR OTHER THIIIIIINGS?
DIIIID YOU HEAR THE OTHER VOIIIIICES?

WHAT'S HE TALKING ABOUT?
THEY...AHEM, WE--YOU SEE, THE BLACK PRIESTS ARE CAUGHT UP IN A CONFLICT THEY WERE NEVER INTENDED TO BE PART OF.
THERE IS A WAR UNDERWAY BETWEEN TWO SEPARATE FORCES: THE IVORY KINGS AND RABUM ALAL.
FROM WHAT I HAVE WITNESSED FIRSTHAND, THEY BOTH WANT THE SAME THING--AND IT'S THE SAME REASON YOU ARE HERE--THE DESTRUCTION OF EVERYTHING.
I KNOW.
THE SEARCH FOR DEATH WITHOUT THE PROMISE OF NEW LIFE OR REBIRTH IS A GREAT SIN IN THE EYES OF THE UNIVERSE.
THEN WHY DO YOU SEEK IT AS WELL?
STEPHEN, I KNOW NOT HOW LONG YOU'VE BEEN GONE FROM EARTH--BUT YOU DISAPPEARED SOME TIME AGO...
THE ACTIONS OF THE ILLUMINATI ARE NOW KNOWN.
WE HAVE SEEN THE RECORDS...THESE PRIESTS--YOU, IF YOU ARE TRULY AMONG THEM--HAVE DESTROYED WORLDS.
OR AM I WRONG?
YOU ARE NOT.
BUT YOU MISUNDERSTAND WHAT WE ARE DOING. THE BLACK PRIESTS ARE THE FIELD SURGEONS OF THE MULTIVERSE.
WE SEEK OUT EARTHS, AS THEY ARE THE TOUCHPOINT OF THE COLLAPSE, AND ELIMINATE THEM... THEREBY SAVING AN ENTIRE UNIVERSE.
WHAT WE DO IS NOT SIMPLE MURDER...IT'S TRIAGE.
AND WE BELIEVE THAT IF WE DESTROY ENOUGH EARTHS, THEN WE CAN STABILIZE ALL OF IT, INCLUDING THE COLLECTIVE HEAT DEATH OF THE UNIVERSE.
WE CAN SAVE EVERYTHING.
UNDERSTAND? EVERYTHING.
THAT IS WHAT THIS POWER IS--THE WORDS ARE LIFE SURROUNDED BY NOTHING BUT DEATH.
DO YOU KNOW WHAT WORD WE USE TO DESTROY A WORLD EACH AND EVERY TIME WE DO IT? "LIFE."

SO EACH PRIEST HAS A LETTER AND TOGETHER THEY MAKE A WORD... WHICH IS, WHAT, LIKE CASTING A SPELL?
OF A SORT. IT'S MORE LIKE A SYMBOL WHICH MEANS "SOMETHING," BUT THE MEANING CHANGES WITH EACH SYMBOL YOU ADD TO IT.
IN CODE-BREAKING TERMS, IT'S ACTUALLY AKIN TO A REPLACEMENT CIPHER.
BUT BACK THERE YOU DIDN'T NEED THE OTHERS TO MAKE **YOUR** WORDS.
NO.
HOW IS THAT POSSIBLE THEN?
I AM THE ***SORCERER SUPREME,*** YOUNG MAN...
I DO NOT SPEAK ***LETTERS***-- I SPEAK ***WORDS.***
AND I KNOW ***ALL OF THEM.***
SO, THEN... THIS IS **NOT** THE PLACE WE ARE LOOKING FOR...
APPARENTLY NOT...BUT STEPHEN, CAN YOU HELP US FIND WHOEVER IT IS THAT WE NEED TO STOP IN ORDER TO END THIS MADNESS? TIME RUNS SHORT.

ACTUALLY, YOUR TIMING COULD NOT BE BETTER, AS I HAVE CONVINCED MY FELLOW PRIESTS THAT WE ALSO NEED TO STRIKE OUT AGAINST OUR ENEMIES.
AND I HAVE AT MY DISPOSAL A FORMIDABLE NUMBER OF SURGEONS.
HOW DO YOU KNOW WHERE TO FIND THEM? HOW DO YOU KNOW WHERE TO LOOK?
TO FIIIIND THE KIIIINGS YOU'LL NEED A MAP-- FIIIIND A MAPMAKER AND YOU'LL FIIIIND THE KIIIINGS.
TO FIIIIND RABUM ALAL, WATCH THE SWANS FLY SOUTH FOR THE WIIIIINTER. THEN SHOOT THEM FROM THE AIIIIIR AND HAVE THEM FOR DIIIIINNER.
SMACK. SMACK. SMACK.
YOU KNOW WHAT I'M THINKING?
DOUBLE OUR CHANCES. YOU GUYS HIT ONE, WE HIT THE OTHER.
THAT'S NOT ACTUALLY DOUBLING YOUR CHANCES, KEVIN. IF YOU WERE GOING TO DOUBLE YOUR CHANCES, THAT WOULD MEAN YOU NEED TO--
SHUT UP, ADAM.
ACCORDING TO WHAT YOU'VE TOLD US, WE HAVE TO STOP *BOTH* IF WE'RE GOING TO BE SUCCESSFUL, RIGHT?
YES.

THEN WE HIT BOTH. AS HARD AND LONG AS WE CAN. UNTIL WE CAN STAND NO MORE...
OR UNTIL WE FALL.
AGREED, BUT WHICH ONE OF--
ALL OF YOU...WATCH THIS:
THE CEPHINZ CRYSTALLINE STRUCTURE IS UNIQUE IN ALL OF THE UNIVERSE FOR ITS LACK OF A MULTIFACETED NATURE.
IT'S PERFECTLY PLANAR, HAVING JUST TWO SIDES--ONE THAT COMPLETELY ABSORBS THE FULL SPECTRUM OF LIGHT, AND THE OTHER, REFLECTING IT.
WE ARE YOUR GUESTS, SORCERER SUPREME, AND IT IS WITH YOUR KNOWLEDGE THAT WE WILL FIND WHAT WE SEEK--PERHAPS IT IS ONLY FITTING THAT WE LEAVE THE CHOICE TO YOU.
SO...
YOU KILL THE IVORY KINGS.
YOU KILL RABUM ALAL.
LET CHAOS BE YOUR GUIDE...
AND CALL IT IN THE AIR.

"YOU CAN'T WIN" PART I

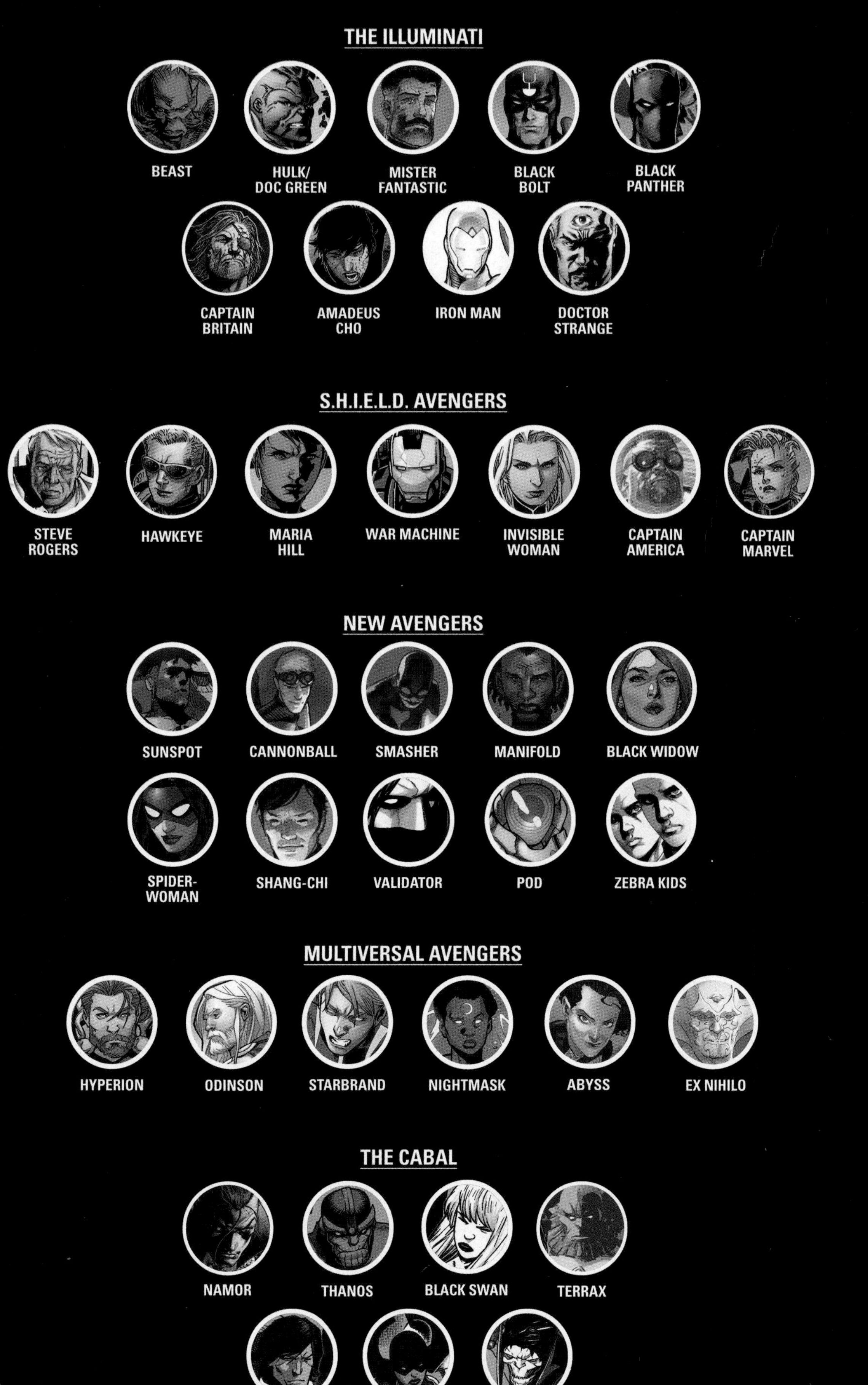
THE ILLUMINATI
BEAST
HULK/ DOC GREEN
MISTER FANTASTIC
BLACK BOLT
BLACK PANTHER
CAPTAIN BRITAIN
AMADEUS CHO
IRON MAN
DOCTOR STRANGE
S.H.I.E.L.D. AVENGERS
STEVE ROGERS
HAWKEYE
MARIA HILL
WAR MACHINE
INVISIBLE WOMAN
CAPTAIN AMERICA
CAPTAIN MARVEL
NEW AVENGERS
SUNSPOT
CANNONBALL
SMASHER
MANIFOLD
BLACK WIDOW
SPIDER-WOMAN
SHANG-CHI
VALIDATOR
POD
ZEBRA KIDS
MULTIVERSAL AVENGERS
HYPERION
ODINSON
STARBRAND
NIGHTMASK
ABYSS
EX NIHILO
THE CABAL
NAMOR
THANOS
BLACK SWAN
TERRAX
MAXIMUS
PROXIMA MIDNIGHT
CORVUS GLAIVE

ILLUMINATI SAFEHOUSE.
CADIZ, SPAIN.
THE PERSONAL LOG OF REED RICHARDS. RECORDING...
MY DEAREST VALERIA...
TODAY, I AM FILLED WITH REGRETS, BUT I'VE SO VERY LITTLE TIME FOR THEM.
ALMOST NONE AT ALL.
Dad,
You can't win.
Time to start figuring out how not to lose.
V
Val

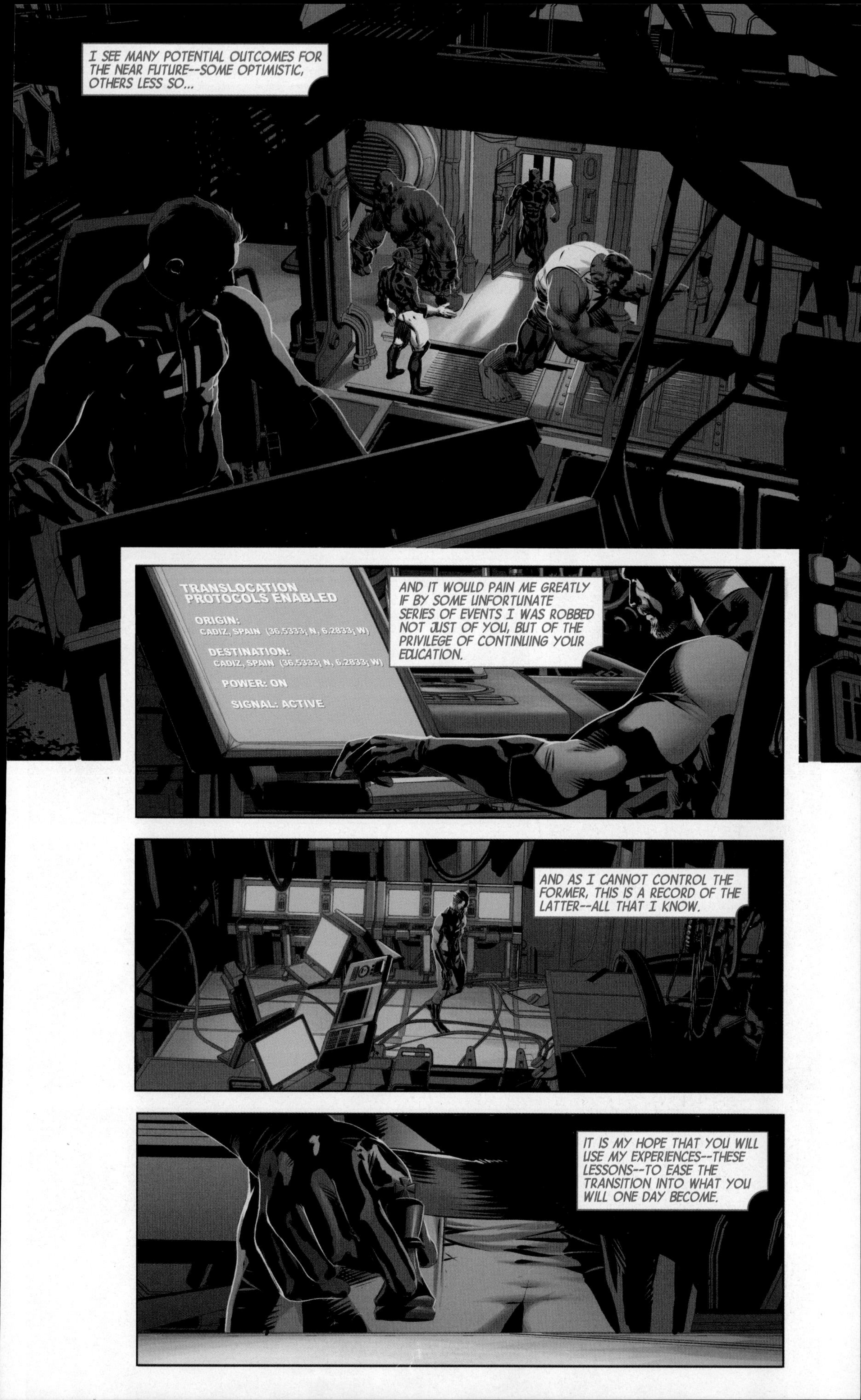
I SEE MANY POTENTIAL OUTCOMES FOR THE NEAR FUTURE--SOME OPTIMISTIC, OTHERS LESS SO...
TRANSLOCATION PROTOCOLS ENABLED
ORIGIN:
CADIZ, SPAIN (36.5333; N, 6.2833; W)
DESTINATION:
CADIZ, SPAIN (36.5333; N, 6.2833; W)
POWER: ON
SIGNAL: ACTIVE
AND IT WOULD PAIN ME GREATLY IF BY SOME UNFORTUNATE SERIES OF EVENTS I WAS ROBBED NOT JUST OF YOU, BUT OF THE PRIVILEGE OF CONTINUING YOUR EDUCATION.
AND AS I CANNOT CONTROL THE FORMER, THIS IS A RECORD OF THE LATTER--ALL THAT I KNOW.
IT IS MY HOPE THAT YOU WILL USE MY EXPERIENCES--THESE LESSONS--TO EASE THE TRANSITION INTO WHAT YOU WILL ONE DAY BECOME.

IT IS MY EVERY EXPECTATION THAT YOU WILL BE SOMETHING MUCH MORE THAN I WAS.

ALWAYS ENDEAVOR TO BE YOUR VERY BEST.
ENGAGE

SO THEN, WE BEGIN WITH YOUR FIRST LESSON:

TRACKING...
MAKING PLANS AND THE PROPER EXECUTION THEREOF.

WE'VE GOT A HIT.
ARCHANGEL HELICARRIER WING.
LOCATED IN THE MEDITERRANEAN.
TRANSLOCATED SIGNAL. TRIANGULATING... IBERIAN PENINSULA.
NARROWING...
SOMEWHERE ON THE COAST OF SPAIN. LOOKS LIKE...
CADIZ. THEY'RE IN CADIZ.
THEY'RE IN RANGE, SIR!
OKAY.
DEPLOY THE DRONES. LET'S GO GET THEM.

SIGNAL LOCKED.
INCOMING
AH! THERE YOU ARE.
I SEE YOU, STEVE.
THEY'RE ON THE WAY.
YOU SENT THE SIGNAL?
I HAD TO-- ALL THE EXTERNAL FACTORS WE TALKED ABOUT WERE ALIGNED. AND WE'RE NOW OFFICIALLY ON THE CLOCK.
HENRY, IS EVERYTHING IN PLACE?
IT IS INDEED.
THEN WE NEED TO MOVE INTO POSITION... CERTAIN PEOPLE WILL BE EXPECTING A SHOW.
AND SO IT STARTS...

ARCHANGEL COMMAND CENTER.
ETA: FOUR MINUTES.
THE DRONES WE LAUNCHED GOT THERE BEFORE A SECOND TRANSLOCATION SIGNAL WAS IDENTIFIED.
A GENERAL NULL FIELD HAS BEEN ERECTED, AND THE DRONES ARE PROGRAMED WITH DNA TRACKING--IF THE TARGETS MOVE, SO WILL THE FIELD.
THEY CAN FIGHT THEIR WAY OUT OF THERE... BUT NOT BEFORE WE ARRIVE.
DOESN'T TRACK...
THEY KNEW WE'D STILL BE IN THE VICINITY AFTER THEY JUMPED FROM ROME. NO WAY THEY'RE DUMB ENOUGH TO DO IT AGAIN SO SOON.
I THINK IT'S A TRAP.
WHAT ABOUT YOU, STEVE?
ME?
CLEVER BOYS BEING OH SO DAMN CLEVER...
I KNOW IT'S A TRAP.

ARCHANGEL WAR MACHINE OPS.
I'M WORRIED THIS IS GOING TO BE TOO MUCH.
YOU SAYING I CAN'T HANDLE IT?
I'M SAYING, RHODEY, THAT I REMEMBER YOU TELLING ME WHAT KIND OF HEADACHE THIS THING GAVE YOU WHEN YOU PRACTICED RUNNING TEN WAR MACHINES.
AND BY HEADACHE, I MEAN THAT...PLUS THE PRETTY FIERCE NOSEBLEED.
THIS IS... MORE.

I'LL BE FINE, CAROL. THE CONTROL SEAT HAS AN AUTO-SHUTDOWN IF PERMANENT DAMAGE IS IMMINENT.
UH-HUH. BECAUSE THAT'S HOW TONY BUILT IT.
YES. BECAUSE THAT'S HOW HE DID IT BACK IN THE DAY...
BUT I DON'T WANT TO TALK ABOUT THAT. I WANT TO HEAR WHO'S ON DECK. YOU GONNA HAVE PROPER BACKUP? BECAUSE IT'S A CONCERN.
WE'LL BE MISSING THE PERSONNEL WHO CYCLED OFF DUTY.
COUPLE PSI-AGENTS. VICTOR WITH THE SECONDARY TEAM. SUSAN WITH THE PRIMARY.
OKAY. WELL, ROTATION GETS THE BEST OF ANY SOLDIER... BUT BE CAREFUL. DNA LOCKS WILL CONFIRM THE MAIN CULPRITS, BUT BE READY FOR ANYTHING...
AND REMEMBER, EVEN IF IT ALL GOES EXACTLY AS PLANNED...THERE'S STILL A HULK DOWN THERE.
YEAH. I KNOW.
I'M GONNA KNOCK HIS ASS OUT.

TWO MINUTES LATER.
LAUNCH.

ENTERING COMBAT AREA.
ENGAGING HOSTILE FORCES.
SCANNING.
TARGET LOCATION ACQUIRED. TARGET SIGNAL SEARCHING...
SCANNING...
SCANNING...
SOMETHING'S NOT RIGHT.
WE'RE RIGHT ON TOP OF... OH...OH, NO...
ALERT.
SEISMIC ACTIVITY.
TARGET LOCATED.
CRAP.

I THINK IT'S IMPORTANT THAT WE BEGIN WITH THE IDEOLOGICAL UNDERPINNINGS OF EXECUTING PROPER GAME THEORY.
WHICH IS, I SUPPOSE, A CUMBERSOME WAY OF SAYING, "KNOW WHO YOU ARE, VALERIA," AS YOUR PERSONALITY WILL DEFINE HOW YOU NATURALLY CONSTRUCT A PLAN.

FOR EXAMPLE: IT'S BEEN SAID MANY TIMES THAT IF YOU WAIT FOR ALL THE INFORMATION NECESSARY TO MAKE A CORRECT DECISION, THE OPPORTUNITY TO MAKE ANY DECISION AT ALL MIGHT HAVE PASSED YOU BY.

OKAY. I THINK THEY'RE SUITABLY DISTRACTED.
YOU CAN COME OUT NOW.

OF COURSE, THE OPPOSITE OF THAT IDEA IS THE UNCOMPLICATED MAXIM: GO WITH YOUR GUT.

THE ARGUMENT THERE BEING "INSTINCT IS AN EVOLUTIONARY GOOD BET"--WHICH IS TRUE, UNTIL YOU RUN INTO SOMETHING, OR SOMEONE, A LITTLE HIGHER UP THE FOOD CHAIN...
OR, IN SOME INSTANCES, MAYBE JUST A BIT MORE HUNGRY.

MOST PEOPLE--EVEN GIFTED ONES LIKE YOURSELF--TEND TO FAVOR ONE OF THESE TWO PRINCIPLES, BUT THE BEST COURSE OF ACTION IS AN AMALGAMATION...
AR

MAINTAINING A CONSTANT AWARENESS OF BOTH CONCEPTS AND WAITING TO ACT UNTIL THE MOMENT THEY INTERSECT--WAITING UNTIL BOTH INSTINCT AND INTELLECT COLLIDE.
TO PUT IT BLUNTLY, WHAT YOU'RE LOOKING FOR IS A PLAN THAT CAN BE EXECUTED WITH PRECISION, BUT ALSO IMPLEMENTED ATEMPORALLY.
MINIMIZE VARIABLES. MAXIMIZE FLEXIBILITY.

WE'RE LOSING TOO MANY UNITS!
I NEED HELP DOWN THERE!

HOW MUCH LONGER CAN RHODEY HOLD OUT?
LESS THAN A MINUTE.
AND HOW LONG UNTIL WE'RE DIRECTLY OVER THE DROP SITE?
LONGER THAN THAT.
AS LONG AS THEY'VE GOT THE HULK--AND UNTIL WE'RE IN POSITION--WE'VE GOT TO HOLD OFF AS LONG AS WE CAN...
YOU THINK THE TWO OF YOU CAN HELP US WITH THAT?
ABSOLUTELY.
INCOMING, YOU MONSTER.
HUH?
BA-BOOOOOM

NEED A HAND?
NO, CLINT. I GOT THIS.
SURE.
BETTER YOU THAN ME.

UH-HUH.

FEEL BETTER?
EXITING THE ATMOSPHERE-- WE JUST LOST CAROL.
WE JUST NEED THIRTY MORE SECONDS.
ANOTHER THING YOU NEED TO CONSIDER IS CONSISTENCY OF DISPOSITION.
CAN YOU REMAIN CALM WHILE EXECUTING YOUR PLAN? THE ANSWER TO THIS MUST ALWAYS BE YES.

PSYCHOLOGICAL WARFARE IS THE TOOL MOST OFTEN USED BY ANYONE STANDING IN OPPOSITION TO YOU ACHIEVING YOUR GOALS. MANIPULATION, ULTIMATUMS, THE THREAT OF PHYSICAL OR EMOTIONAL HARM...THESE ARE TOOLS OF RESISTANCE.
AND WHILE THEY MAY NOT BE SUFFICIENT TO STOP YOU, LIKE BARNACLES ON A SHIP, THEY ARE ENOUGH TO CAUSE DRAG AND PUT YOUR GOALS IN PERIL. YOU MUST AT ALL TIMES MAINTAIN COMPOSURE.
NOW I WANT TO WARN YOU, VALERIA, THERE ARE THOSE WHO WILL NOT UNDERSTAND THIS DISPASSION. THEY WILL CALL YOU COLD AND UNFEELING... WHICH IS UNTRUE.
I CAN'T GET THROUGH... THE MOBILE NULL FIELD--
AH, YES...OKAY. RECALIBRATING YOUR COMM.
BE-DOOP
THAT SHOULD DO IT, HENRY. NOW YOU CAN--
ARRGH!
HURK!
WE FEEL AS MUCH AS ANYONE. WE HURT. WE CRY.
BUT WE KEEP IT IN CHECK UNTIL... LATER.

ARE WE GOING TO HAVE A PROBLEM HERE, BOYS...
OR CAN WE FINALLY PUT A QUIET END TO THIS GAME OF CHASE?
HAPPY TO COMPLY, CLINT. BUT I DON'T THINK DOCTOR RICHARDS AND I ARE THE ONES YOU SHOULD BE WORRIED ABOUT.
BZZTTT
MESSAGE RECEIVED.
STEVE, I'VE GOT REED AND THE BEAST UNDER WRAPS, BUT CAPTAIN BRITAIN, BLACK PANTHER AND THE HULK ARE ALMOST DONE WITH THE WAR MACHINES AND ARE ABOUT TO BECOME A BIG PROBLEM.
PLEASE ADVISE.
STAND BY, CLINT.
MARIA, ARE WE THERE?
YES, SIR. IN POSITION.
OKAY, SEND IN--
WE'VE GOT A PROBLEM!

WHAT IN THE...

AND FINALLY WE COME TO STRATEGY-- HOW TO ACHIEVE YOUR GOALS.

I WON'T BOTHER GOING INTO LIMITED SCENARIOS FOR CLEARLY DEFINED OPPONENTS OR SITUATIONS. THESE ARE SIMPLE AND YOU ARE WELL BEYOND NEEDING YOUR FATHER'S ADVICE ON HANDLING THOSE...

ATTENTION: AGENTS OF S.H.I.E.L.D.

BUT WHEN FACING A WELL-SEASONED OR TRULY GIFTED OPPONENT, YOU MUST ALWAYS ATTEMPT TO REDEFINE YOUR OPPONENT'S BASE UNDERSTANDING OF THE ENCOUNTER.

YOU ATTACK THEIR PRIMARY HYPOTHESES.

FOR EXAMPLE: IF THERE IS AN EXPECTATION THAT A CONFLICT IS BETWEEN TWO PARTIES-- ONE OF THEM BEING YOURS...

THE FIRST THING YOU DO...
IS INTRODUCE A THIRD.
THIS IS THE AVENGERS ORDERING YOU TO STAND DOWN.

S.H.I.E.L.D. AVENGERS
STEVE ROGERS
HAWKEYE
MARIA HILL
WAR MACHINE
INVISIBLE WOMAN
CAPTAIN AMERICA
CAPTAIN MARVEL
THE ILLUMINATI
BEAST
HULK/ DOC GREEN
REED RICHARDS
BLACK BOLT
BLACK PANTHER
CAPTAIN BRITAIN
AMADEUS CHO
IRON MAN
DOCTOR STRANGE
NEW AVENGERS
SUNSPOT
CANNONBALL
SMASHER
MANIFOLD
BLACK WIDOW
SPIDER-WOMAN
SHANG-CHI
VALIDATOR
POD
ZEBRA KIDS
MULTIVERSAL AVENGERS
HYPERION
ODINSON
STARBRAND
NIGHTMASK
ABYSS
EX NIHILO
THE CABAL
NAMOR
THANOS
BLACK SWAN
TERRAX
MAXIMUS
PROXIMA MIDNIGHT
CORVUS GLAIVE

CADIZ, SPAIN.
THE AIRSPACE ABOVE AN ILLUMINATI SAFEHOUSE.
I KNOW WHAT YOU'RE THINKING...
WHY IN THE WORLD WOULD SOMEONE AS HANDSOME AS I EVER BOTHER TO STICK THIS GLORIOUS MUG IN THE MIDDLE OF WHAT IS, NO DOUBT, A VERY PERSONAL AND VIOLENT AFFAIR.
WELL, STEVE... IT'S A QUESTION THAT HAS A VERY SIMPLE ANSWER.

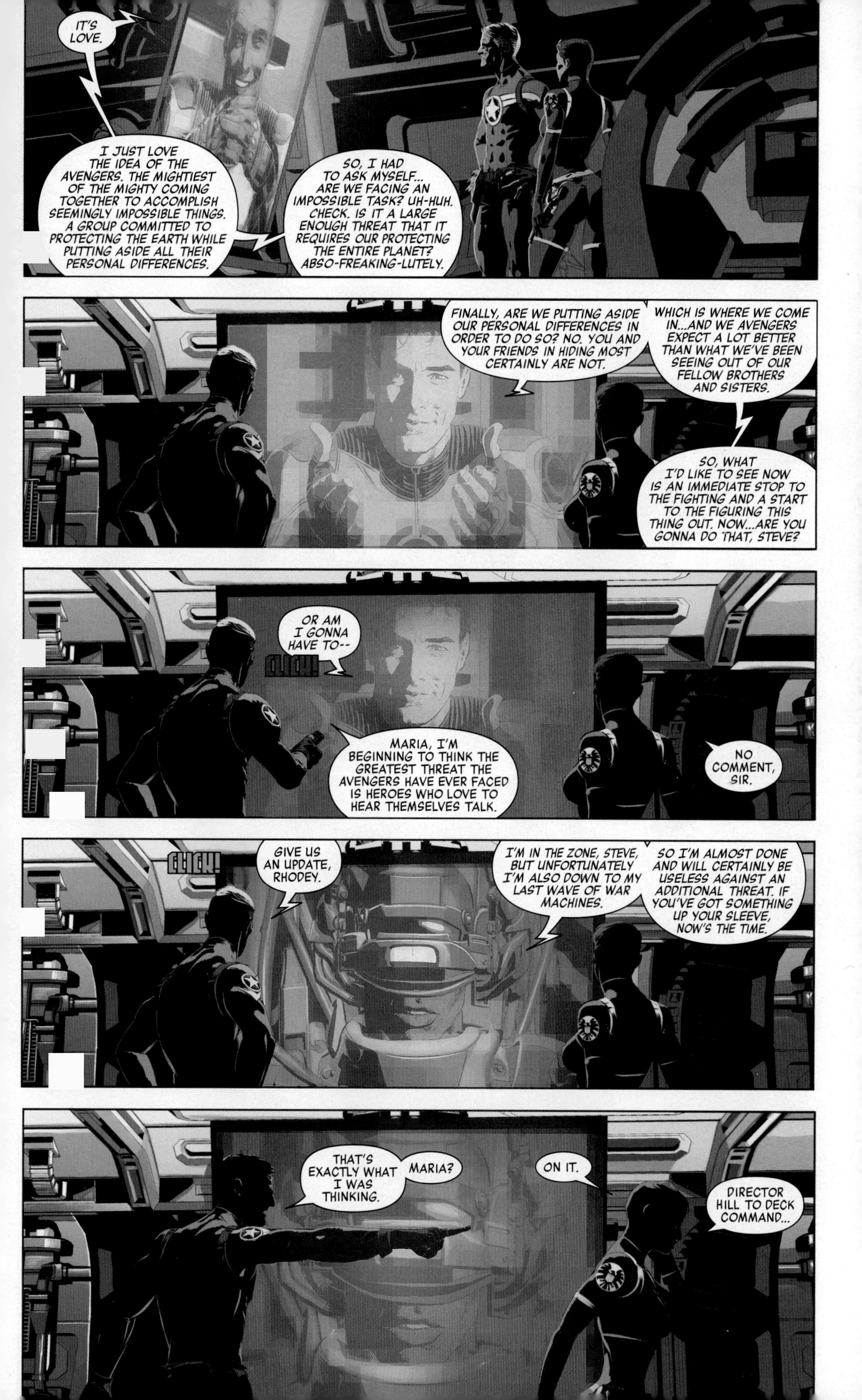
IT'S LOVE.
I JUST LOVE THE IDEA OF THE AVENGERS. THE MIGHTIEST OF THE MIGHTY COMING TOGETHER TO ACCOMPLISH SEEMINGLY IMPOSSIBLE THINGS. A GROUP COMMITTED TO PROTECTING THE EARTH WHILE PUTTING ASIDE ALL THEIR PERSONAL DIFFERENCES.
SO, I HAD TO ASK MYSELF... ARE WE FACING AN IMPOSSIBLE TASK? UH-HUH. CHECK. IS IT A LARGE ENOUGH THREAT THAT IT REQUIRES OUR PROTECTING THE ENTIRE PLANET? ABSO-FREAKING-LUTELY.
FINALLY, ARE WE PUTTING ASIDE OUR PERSONAL DIFFERENCES IN ORDER TO DO SO? NO. YOU AND YOUR FRIENDS IN HIDING MOST CERTAINLY ARE NOT.
WHICH IS WHERE WE COME IN...AND WE AVENGERS EXPECT A LOT BETTER THAN WHAT WE'VE BEEN SEEING OUT OF OUR FELLOW BROTHERS AND SISTERS.
SO, WHAT I'D LIKE TO SEE NOW IS AN IMMEDIATE STOP TO THE FIGHTING AND A START TO THE FIGURING THIS THING OUT. NOW...ARE YOU GONNA DO THAT, STEVE?
OR AM I GONNA HAVE TO--
CLICK!
MARIA, I'M BEGINNING TO THINK THE GREATEST THREAT THE AVENGERS HAVE EVER FACED IS HEROES WHO LOVE TO HEAR THEMSELVES TALK.
NO COMMENT, SIR.
CLICK!
GIVE US AN UPDATE, RHODEY.
I'M IN THE ZONE, STEVE, BUT UNFORTUNATELY I'M ALSO DOWN TO MY LAST WAVE OF WAR MACHINES.
SO I'M ALMOST DONE AND WILL CERTAINLY BE USELESS AGAINST AN ADDITIONAL THREAT. IF YOU'VE GOT SOMETHING UP YOUR SLEEVE, NOW'S THE TIME.
THAT'S EXACTLY WHAT I WAS THINKING.
MARIA?
ON IT.
DIRECTOR HILL TO DECK COMMAND...

"DEPLOY THE PACKAGE."
OKAY, IT'S TIME.
LET'S GO.
YOU SHOULDN'T BE DOING THIS.
IT'S WRONG.
ORDERS ARE ORDERS, PAL. AND IF YOU DON'T MIND ME SAYING...
IF YOU REALLY FELT THAT WAY, I THINK YOU'D BE A LITTLE MORE OUTRAGED.
I DON'T REALLY HAVE A CHOICE IN THE MATTER.
WELL, US EITHER.
OFF YOU GO.
HELLO, DOCTOR, YOU MUST BE GETTING TIRED OF SITTING IN THAT CELL ALL DAY, EVERY DAY.
HOW WOULD YOU LIKE TO TAKE A TRIP? GET OUTSIDE? MAYBE GET A LITTLE EXERCISE?
SOUNDS GREAT, I SAID. ANY CHANCE OF SOME DECENT SCENERY. SOMETHING OF A VIEW?
OH, THEY SAID. IT'LL TAKE YOUR BREATH AWAY.
SIGH.
DIRECTOR HILL...
PACKAGE DEPLOYED.

PACKAGE ON ITS WAY, STEVE.
BUT I GOTTA ASK, SHOULDN'T I FEEL A BIT GUILTY ABOUT JUST THROWING A GUY OFF THE SIDE OF A HELICARRIER?
HIS ALTERNATE-WORLD GENOCIDAL AVENGERS CAME HERE FROM AN EARTH THEY CONQUERED, MARIA.
NO, I DON'T FEEL BAD.
SYSTEM ARMED.
"IN FACT, I THINK THE ACTIONS OF OUR FRIENDS DOWN THERE ABSOLUTELY MERIT A RUN-IN WITH AN EMOTIONALLY NEUTERED, SOCIOPATH BANNER.
"MAKING THAT HAPPEN IS JUST A MATTER OF SIGNALING HIS IMPLANTED CONTROL NODE.
"AND I GOT NO PROBLEM FLIPPING THAT SWITCH."
"SYSTEM ACTIVATED."

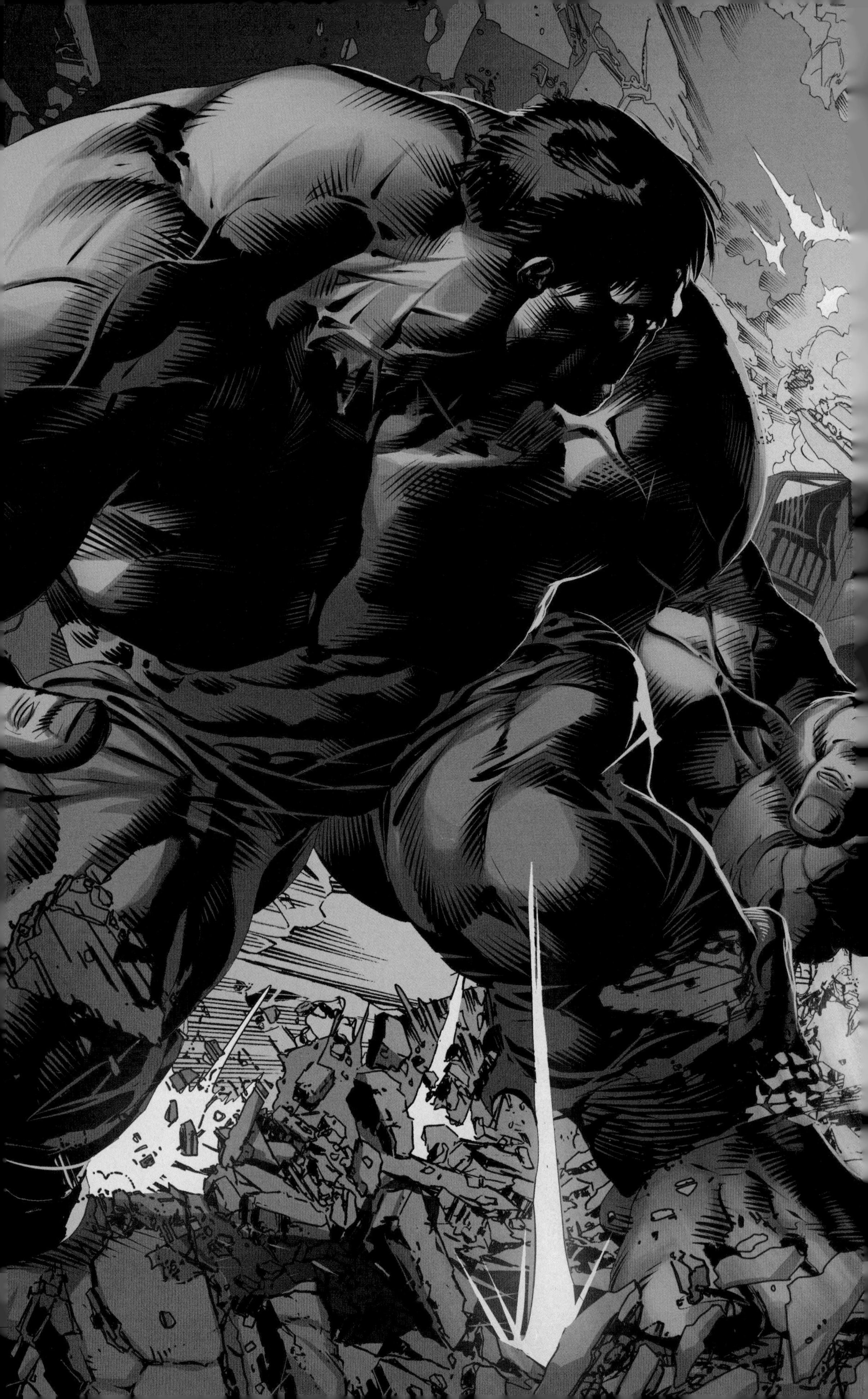

WHOA.
YEAH. SEISMOLOGISTS ALL OVER THE PLANET ARE HAVING A FIELD DAY RIGHT NOW...
BUT IT'S THE BREATHER WE NEEDED. RETASK ALL AVAILABLE S.H.I.E.L.D. PERSONNEL TO HANDLE DA COSTA'S TEAM, WHILE WE--
FWASSSHHH!
WHAT THE--
HELLO, STEVE.
ANY CHANCE YOU MIGHT BE MORE OPEN TO ENDING THIS IF THE REQUEST CAME FROM AN OLD FRIEND?
OLD FRIENDS IS WHAT GOT US HERE, NATASHA.

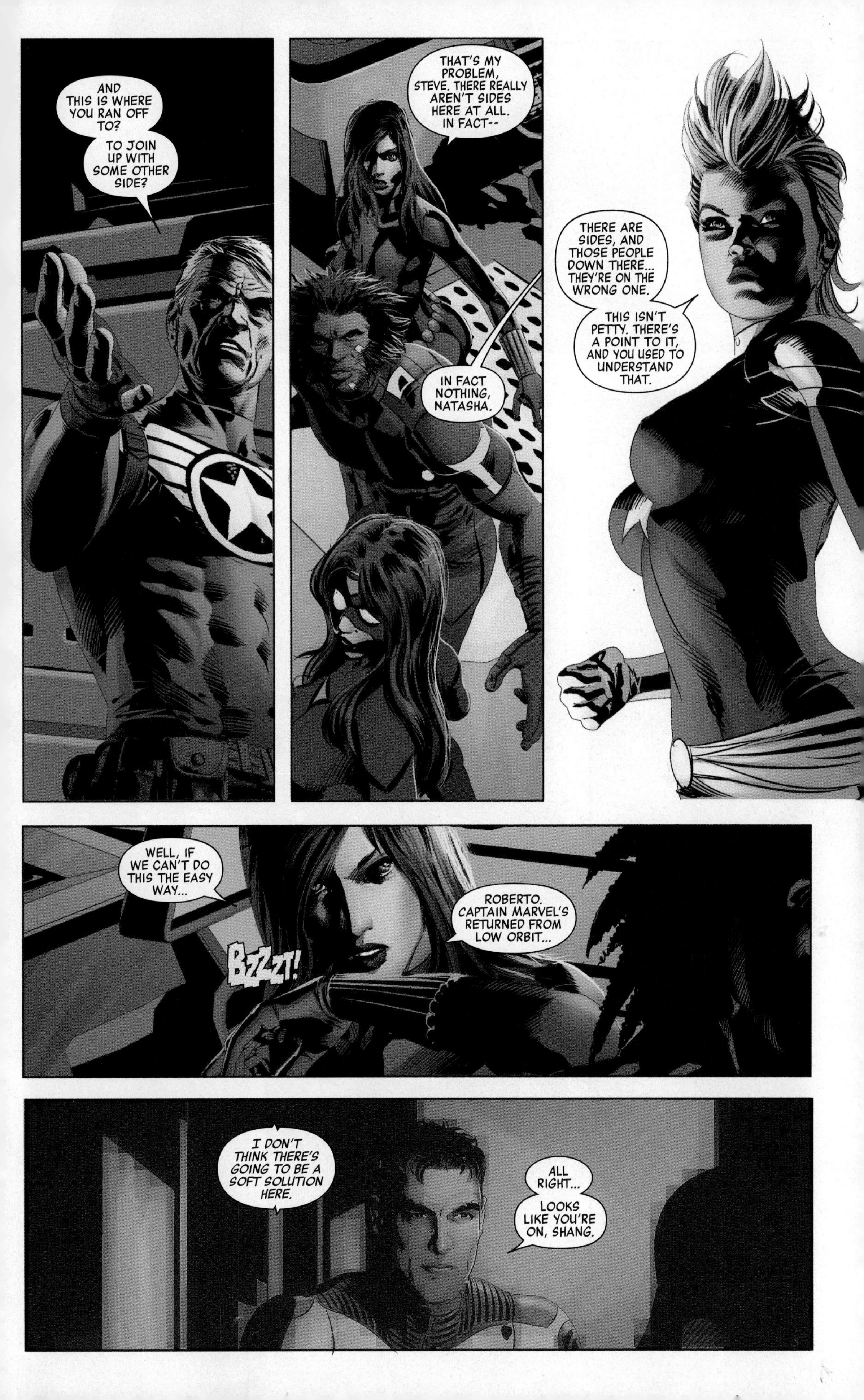
AND THIS IS WHERE YOU RAN OFF TO?
TO JOIN UP WITH SOME OTHER SIDE?
THAT'S MY PROBLEM, STEVE. THERE REALLY AREN'T SIDES HERE AT ALL. IN FACT--
IN FACT NOTHING, NATASHA.
THERE ARE SIDES, AND THOSE PEOPLE DOWN THERE... THEY'RE ON THE WRONG ONE.
THIS ISN'T PETTY. THERE'S A POINT TO IT, AND YOU USED TO UNDERSTAND THAT.
WELL, IF WE CAN'T DO THIS THE EASY WAY...
BZZZT!
ROBERTO. CAPTAIN MARVEL'S RETURNED FROM LOW ORBIT...
I DON'T THINK THERE'S GOING TO BE A SOFT SOLUTION HERE.
ALL RIGHT...
LOOKS LIKE YOU'RE ON, SHANG.

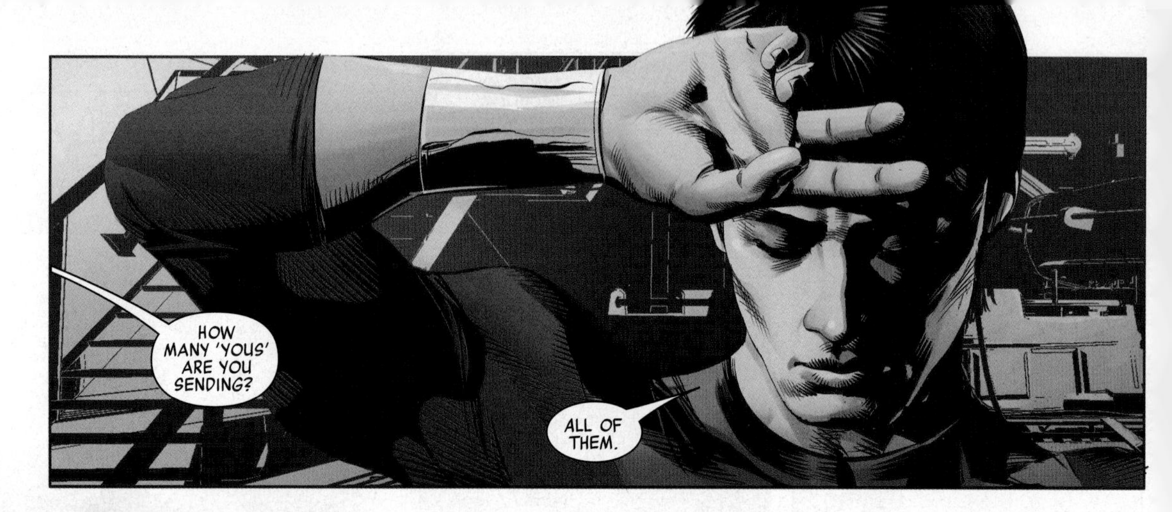
HOW MANY 'YOUS' ARE YOU SENDING?
ALL OF THEM.

GETTING WORD OF SHANG CHI APPEARING ALL OVER THIS CARRIER. MULTIPLE SIGHTINGS, MULTIPLE DECKS.
WE'RE LOSING GROUND FAST. I'M GONNA PREP THE THING FOR THE THING I'M NOT SO HOT ABOUT...

COME ON, STEVE. IT DOESN'T HAVE TO END LIKE THIS.

END?
THIS DOESN'T END UNTIL THEY ANSWER FOR WHAT THEY'VE DONE, NATASHA.
IT DOESN'T WASH OFF. UNDERSTAND?

CAROL...
YEAH?
PLEASE KEEP THESE GOOD PEOPLE FROM GETTING IN THE WAY...

...AS OUR FIGHT'S NOT WITH THEM.

PSSSTTTT!
YOU HAVE THE BRIDGE.
I'M GONNA BE SICK. YOU SURE THIS IS GOING TO WORK?
MOBILE CONTROL UNIT IS ONLINE...
SENDING COMMAND.
"CATCH."
WHHUMP!
NOT GONNA LIE...
I COULD GET USED TO HAVING A FULL-TIME REMOTE-CONTROL HULK.

MIGHT MAKE DAYS LIKE THESE A LITTLE MORE INFREQUENT.
STEVE!
PLEASE! I'M BEGGING YOU. JUST LET US DO WHAT NEEDS TO BE DONE. IT'S NOT TOO LATE...WE THINK THERE ARE STILL OPTIONS--THINGS WE HAVEN'T TRIED.
DON'T MAKE THIS ANY WORSE THAN IT ALREADY IS.
HRMPT!
YOU THERE, SAM?
YES.
OKAY.... READY TO LET THESE PEOPLE IN ON OUR LITTLE SECRET?
UH-HUH. ABOUT TIME.
WHAT NEEDS TO BE DONE, HENRY? YOU PEOPLE AND YOUR BIG IDEAS.
YOU GOT PLANS...WELL, SO DO I.

CAPTAIN AMERICA
LUKE CAGE
WHITE TIGER
SHE-HULK
SPIDER-MAN
BLUE MARVEL
SPECTRUM
POWER MAN
THE PROLONGED OBJECT OF ANY PLAN IS NOT TO GET WHAT YOU WANT, BUT TO DISCOVER WHAT YOUR OPPONENT IS CAPABLE OF.
WHAT YOU ARE INTERESTED IN IS GAUGING THEIR RESPONSE TO YOUR ACTIONS.

WHEN I SPOKE OF CHALLENGING A GIFTED OPPONENT'S PRIMARY HYPOTHESIS, I USED THE EXAMPLE OF DISRUPTING A CONFLICT BETWEEN TWO PARTIES--YOU AND THEM--BY INTRODUCING A THIRD GROUP...
YOUR OPPONENT'S RESPONSE TO THIS WILL INFORM YOUR NEXT ACTION.

FOR INSTANCE, LET US EXAMINE MY RECENT CONFLICT WITHIN THE MULTIFACETED AVENGERS MACHINE AS A TEST CASE FOR EFFECTIVE PLANNING.
STEVE ROGERS' RESPONSE TO THE THIRD-PARTY SCENARIO (THE AVENGERS WORLD TEAM) WAS THE INTRODUCTION OF AN ALT-UNIVERSE HULK ANALOG.
AN EFFECTIVE CHOICE. UNPREDICTABLE. UNEXPECTED.

BUT EVEN GIVEN THAT, IF THE HULK WOULD HAVE BEEN HIS SOLE RESPONSE, IT WOULD HAVE BEEN A FUTILE EFFORT AS HE WOULD HAVE EXPOSED HIS TRUE INTENTIONS TOO EARLY FOR THE NUMBER OF VARIABLES AT PLAY.
BUT THIS IS STEVE ROGERS WE'RE TALKING ABOUT, VALERIA...SO IT WAS NOT.
THE HULK DID SERVE AS AN EXCELLENT BRANCHING SCENARIO, ENABLING CAPTAIN ROGERS TO HOLD DOWN TWO FRONTS (S.H.I.E.L.D. ENGAGED WITH THE AVENGERS WORLD, WHILE HE ENGAGED WITH US).
IN FACT, HAD HE NOT SUFFERED CONSIDERABLE LOSSES MAINTAINING A ZONE OF CONFLICT (PREVENTING US FROM AN EARLY TACTICAL RETREAT VIA TRANSLOCATOR), THE HULK GAMBIT MIGHT HAVE SUCCEEDED IN MAKING US INTRODUCE OUR ASSETS INTO THE FIELD EARLIER THAN DESIRED.

BUT HE DID SUFFER LOSSES, SO HE WAS FORCED TO INTRODUCE A FOURTH PARTY--HIS SECRET AVENGERS.
YOU!

IMMENSELY POWERFUL. TACTICALLY VARIED. AN EXCELLENT STRATEGEM, BUT UNFORTUNATELY FOR HIM, HIS LAST PIECE AVAILABLE ON THE BOARD.

IT'S OVER, RICHARDS!
TIME TO PAY!

HAVEN'T WE ALL PAID ENOUGH THIS TIME?
REMEMBER, AS I SAID EARLIER, THE OBJECT OF ANY PLAN IS NOT TO GET WHAT YOU WANT, BUT TO DISCOVER WHAT YOUR OPPONENT IS CAPABLE OF...

AND ONCE YOU KNOW THAT, YOU CAN MANIPULATE THE BOARD TO ENGINEER, AND MANAGE, A SUCCESSFUL ENDGAME.

WHAT IS...
OH, NO.
THE INVISIBLE WOMAN.
THAT'S RIGHT. DISAPPOINTING I'M SURE...
AND YOU MUST BE WONDERING HOW SHE PULLED IT OFF.
AS YOU PUT IN A LOT OF EFFORT. TRACKING DEVICES. DAILY SCANS...
YOU WERE SO CAREFUL.
BUT WE WERE EVEN MORE SO.

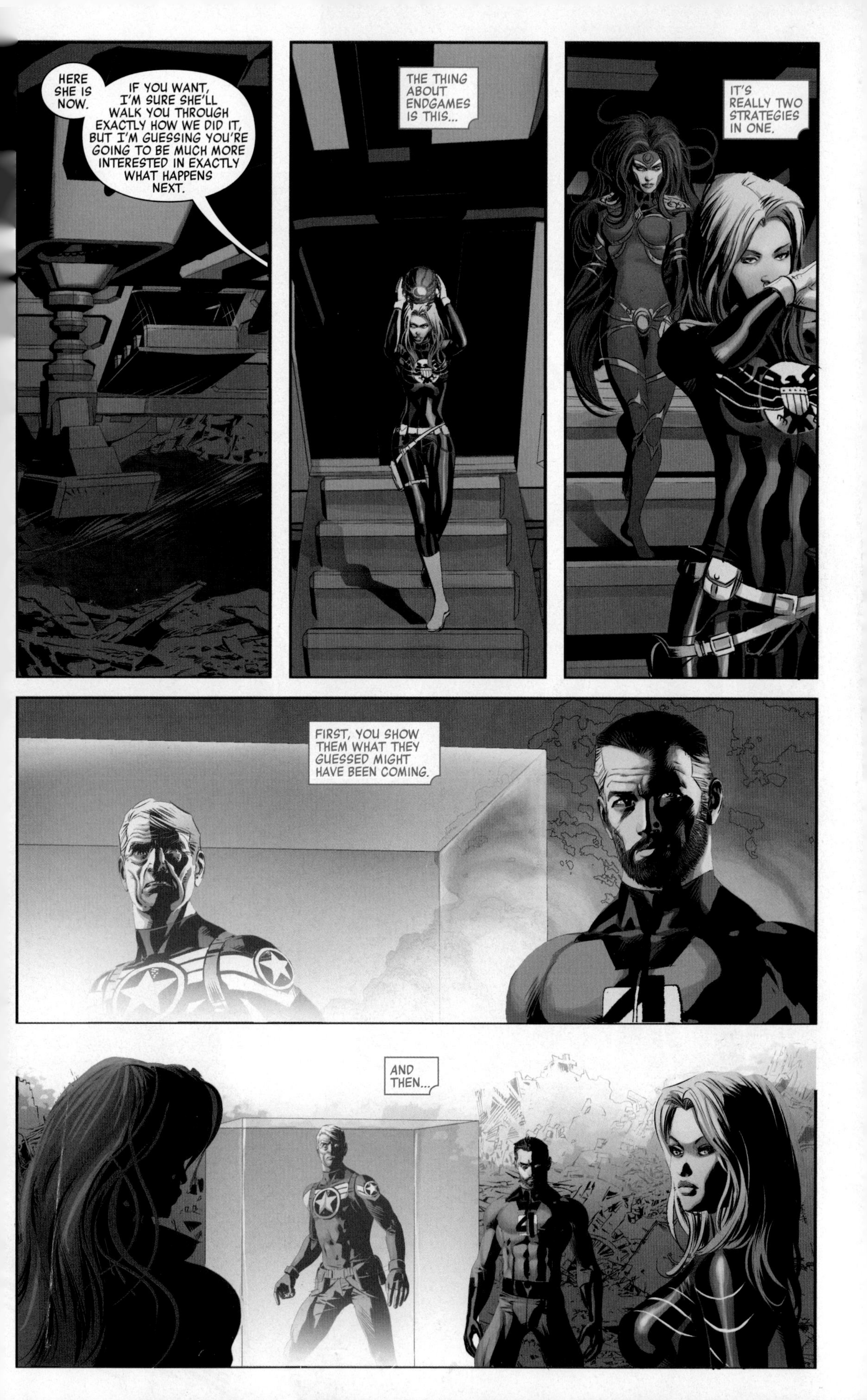
HERE SHE IS NOW.
IF YOU WANT, I'M SURE SHE'LL WALK YOU THROUGH EXACTLY HOW WE DID IT, BUT I'M GUESSING YOU'RE GOING TO BE MUCH MORE INTERESTED IN EXACTLY WHAT HAPPENS NEXT.
THE THING ABOUT ENDGAMES IS THIS...
IT'S REALLY TWO STRATEGIES IN ONE.
FIRST, YOU SHOW THEM WHAT THEY GUESSED MIGHT HAVE BEEN COMING.
AND THEN...

YOU SHOW THEM WHAT THEY DIDN'T.
NEW AVENGERS

COVER GALLERY

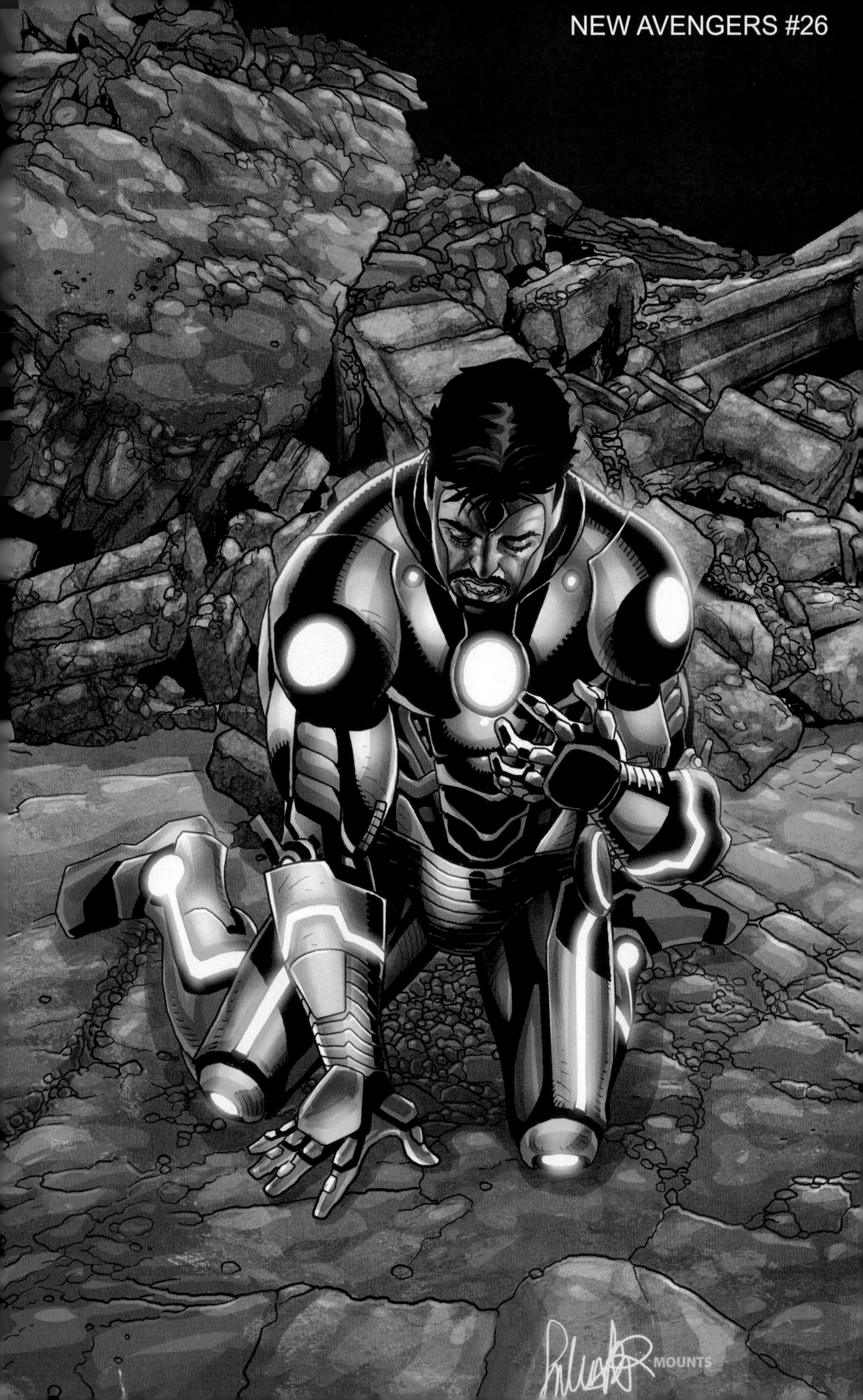
NEW AVENGERS #26
MOUNTS

AVENGERS #38

AVENGERS #39

NEW AVENGERS #28

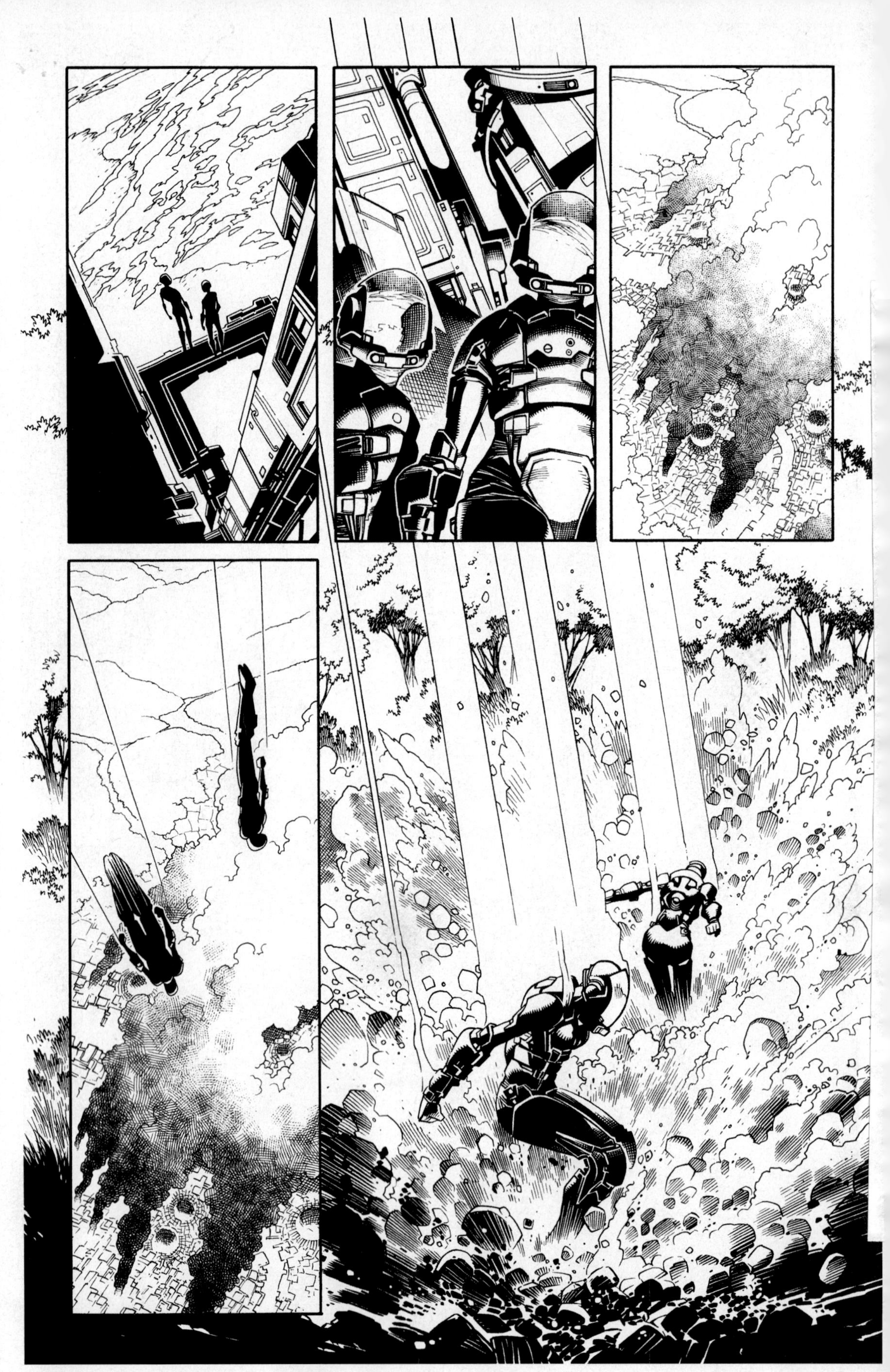

NEW AVENGERS #26, PAGE 1 ART
BY KEV WALKER

NEW AVENGERS #26, PAGE 3 ART
BY KEV WALKER

AVENGERS #38, PAGE 1 ART
BY STEFANO CASELLI

AVENGERS #38, PAGE 4 ART
BY STEFANO CASELLI

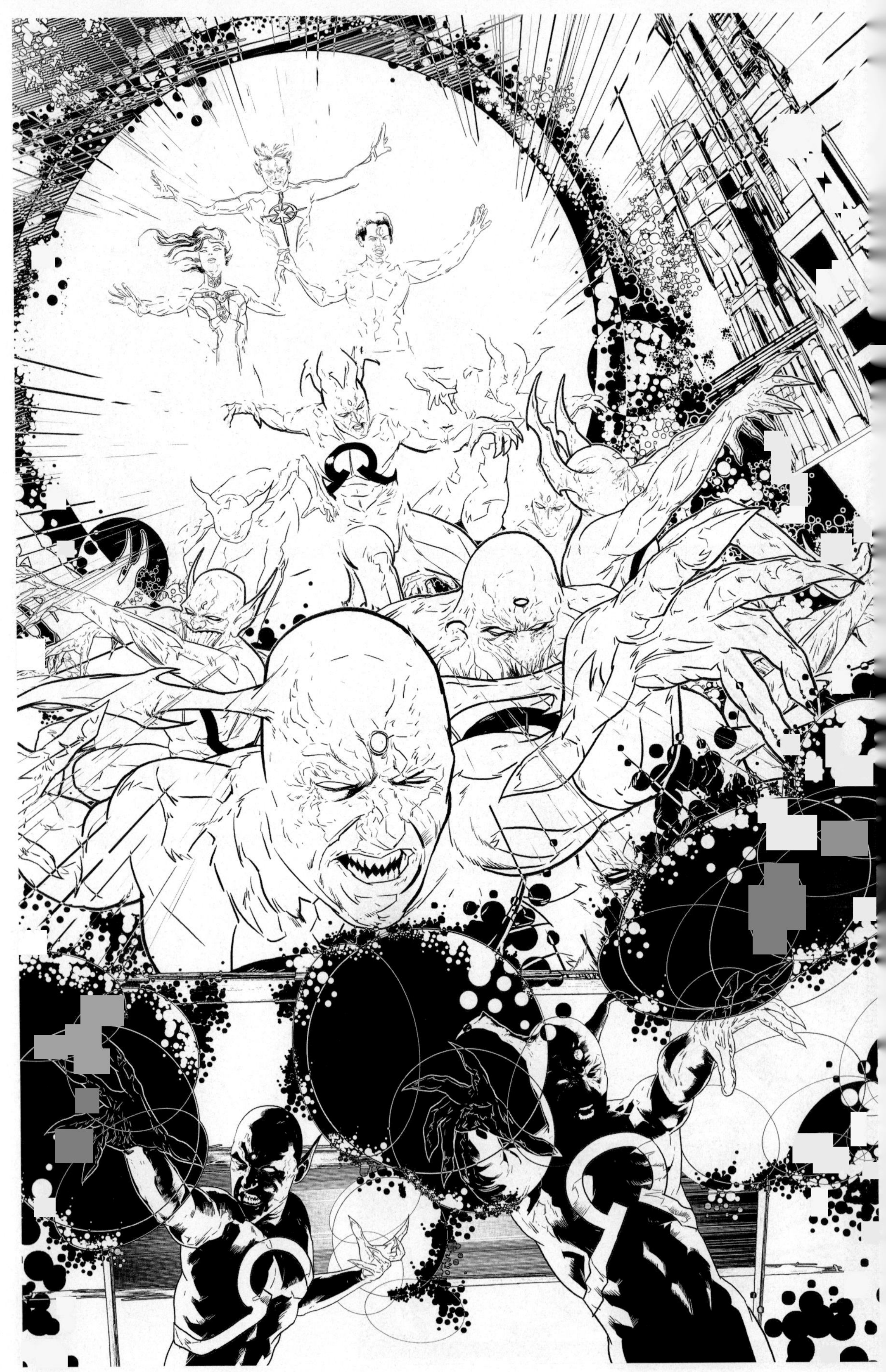

NEW AVENGERS #27, PAGE 2 ART
BY SZYMON KUDRANSKI

NEW AVENGERS #27, PAGE 6 ART
BY SZYMON KUDRANSKI

AVENGERS #39, PAGE 15 ART
BY MIKE DEODATO

NEW AVENGERS #28, PAGE 13 ART
BY MIKE DEODATO

NEW AVENGERS #28, PAGES 5-6 ART
BY MIKE DEODATO

NEW AVENGERS #28, PAGES 14-15 ART
BY MIKE PERKINS

MARVEL AUGMENTED REALITY (AR) ENHANCES AND CHANGES THE WAY YOU EXPERIENCE COMICS!

TO ACCESS THE FREE MARVEL AR CONTENT IN THIS BOOK*:

1. Locate the AR logo within the comic.
2. Go to Marvel.com/AR in your web browser.
3. Search by series title to find the corresponding AR.
4. Enjoy Marvel AR!

*All AR content that appears in this book has been archived and will be available only at Marvel.com/AR – no longer in the Marvel AR App. Content subject to change and availability.

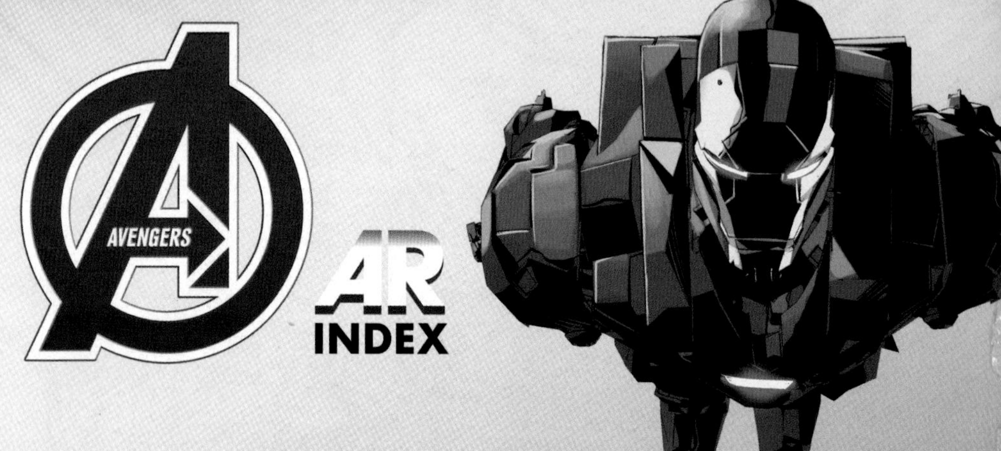

TO REDEEM YOUR CODE FOR A FREE DIGITAL COPY:

1. GO TO MARVEL.COM/REDEEM. OFFER EXPIRES ON 2/25/17.
2. FOLLOW THE ON-SCREEN INSTRUCTIONS TO REDEEM YOUR DIGITAL COPY.
3. LAUNCH THE MARVEL COMICS APP TO READ YOUR COMIC NOW!
4. YOUR DIGITAL COPY WILL BE FOUND UNDER THE *MY COMICS* TAB.
5. READ & ENJOY!

YOUR FREE DIGITAL COPY WILL BE AVAILABLE ON:

MARVEL COMICS APP FOR APPLE® iOS DEVICES

MARVEL COMICS APP FOR ANDROID™ DEVICES